School code kids

Grade six

Tonia Inturrisi

 pencil

ISBN 978-93-5667-359-5
© Tonia Inturrisi 2023
Published in India 2023 by Pencil

A brand of
One Point Six Technologies Pvt. Ltd.
123, Building J2, Shram Seva Premises,
Wadala Truck Terminal, Wadala (E)
Mumbai 400037, Maharashtra, INDIA
E connect@thepencilapp.com
W www.thepencilapp.com

DISCLAIMER: *This is a work of fiction. Names, characters, places, events and incidents are the products of the author's imagination. The opinions expressed in this book do not seek to reflect the views of the Publisher.*

Author biography

My name is Tonia Inturrisi. I am 38 years old, live in Melbourne Australia and have a partner. I enjoy writing, dancing and currently work in hospitality.

CONTENTS

school code kids

School code Special
  School code kids
Book 1-Grade six
  Part 1-Introducing our characters
Chapter 1
Stacey

Hi everyone, my name is Stacey Green and I just turned 11 years old. I go to school at Jefferson primary school in Queensland. I just started grade six and I am a senior at my school and so are my friends. I have gone to the same school since grade prep, and I have had the same friends from when I was 5 years old to now.   I am an only child and am close to my cousins, aunts, uncles, and grandparents. My parents spoil me, since I am their only daughter, although they can be strict. I like -my town, school and friends and I am happy, although I do not have many friends at school and do not play with many girls. I only have a few close friends.

I am your typical 11-year-old active child and am proud of that! I love sports and playing basketball for the school team and socially, swim competitively at school and am always running around after my friends, wrestling, playing sport, playing video games, and riding around on bikes and I like going to the movies too and going out to the playground with my friends and the kids play center. Robert, Shannon, and David are my friends at school and outside school and are my age and are in the same class as me at school. They are my only close friends! Although I do not care, and we like our little group and get along great.

Robert is my best friend. Robert is my age and we have known each other since we were babies and grew up together and are still close.
Robert is a typical 11-year-old boy and loves playing sports, particularly soccer, football and riding bikes and he enjoys video games and watching movies. Robert is cute and has brown hair, brown eyes and curly hair and he is tall for our age and is 5'5 tall and he is still skinny and has not developed muscle yet, but he is only 11 years old.

Robert lives with his parents and has a 3-year-old brother Sal, who is cute. Robert is Italian and come from a large extended family, although they all live in Melbourne, except for Robert's parents and Robert and Sal. Robert's cousins, aunts, uncles, and grandparents live in Melbourne.

Robert and I are close and do everything together. Going to each other's houses, playing at school and he is my best friend! Definitely and I do not care that Robert's a boy and he does not care that I am a girl. Roberts always had no issues having female friends. Robert and I tend to play fight a lot too and I act like a little active child around Robert! It does not take much to start a wrestling match between us! Which is funny, but it is one of our favorite games. Robert's a great guy and we are close, and he can be protective of me and Shannon. Boys know not to tease us at school! Or they have Robert to answer to.

Shannon is my other best friend. Shannon is great and we are inseparable in and out of school and do everything together too and Shannon and Robert are also close. Shannon is pretty with blond hair and blue eyes, and she is short and skinny and like me plays a lot of sport, including netball and she also enjoys soccer, bike riding and video games and like me she is an active child! Shannon and I are proud of that though and do not play with barbie dolls or dance and prefer to play sport, wrestle with Robert and David and are always jumping on the boys and starting wrestling matches and fights and it is very amusing! We match it with them great and Shannon and I play those games with each other too. Shannon is an only child and lives with her parents and has grandparents, but no aunts, uncles, or cousins.

David is also another close friend of ours, although he only moved to town about 2 years ago from Perth. David got close with Robert Shannon, and I quickly thought and is a great guy and he loves playing with us at school and we go to each other's houses too. David is tall already, even at 11 years old, and towers over everyone! At 5'9 and he has not even hit his growth spurt yet! Like Robert has not.

David lives with his parents and his older brother Shane, who is in year 8 at Jefferson Secondary College. David is also sporty and plays rugby and he just started surfing lessons and really enjoys it.

David is close to Robert and before David came along Robert had no male friends, he is close to Shannon and I and did not mind that, but David is a great guy and is good friends with all of us.

So, they are my friends! I know that it is a small group, but I really love Shannon, Robert, and David. We are close and enjoy spending time with each other and the boys are full of fun and always coming up for games for us to play and starting mischief and Shannon and I are close to each other and the boys too.
David is close to Robert and before David came along Robert had no male friends, he is close to Shannon and I and did not mind that, but David is a great guy and is good friends with all of us.

So, they are my friends! I know that it is a small group, but I really love Shannon, Robert, and David. We are close and enjoy spending time with each other and the boys are full of fun and always coming up for games for us to play and starting mischief and Shannon and I are close to each other and the boys too.

Shannon, Robert, and I have been friends forever! Seriously. Or it feels like it. We are family friends, and our parents are close too. We went to childcare, kindergarten, and all primary school together and are still as close as we were when we were little.

At school Shannon and I always prefer hanging out with Robert and David and playing with the boys and have never wanted to join the popular group, although we are on speaking terms with most of the girls in our class and they are always trying to get us to play with them! It is amusing.

In our grade six class at school the popular girls and boys are finally starting to play together! Although that took a while. It is only recently and before this year the girls would play together and the boys had their own group and would even tease the girls and not let them join their games, but some of those girls I think are starting to notice the boys and vice versa.

Sabrina Brewer is the ringleader of the popular girls and Sabrina has always been popular. Sabrina is very girly and does not play sport and has had a large group of girls that she is played with since she was five years old at school. Her main friends are Elise, Grace, Sophie, Emma, Vicky, and Charlotte.

I have nothing against Sabrina and neither does Shannon or Robert. Sabrina lives down the road from me and Shannon and Robert are a couple of streets away. Sabrina comes over to my place to play occasionally, since our mums are friends and she is friends with Robert outside school too, since they live right across the road from each other! Sabrina is not that close a friend to us though and we do not really play together at school, just after school occasionally and Sabrina is closer to Robert then to Shannon or I. Sabrina does not play with Robert at school or did not before this year because the group at school were all girls and they did not invite the boys to play with them.

I do not know! That always seemed silly to me, and Sabrina is friends with all of us, but at school Shannon and I prefer to join Robert and David at recess and lunch for sport, wrestling and just talking. Sabrina did invite Shannon and I to play with the girls at lunch and recess because she said that she feels sorry for us only having Robert and David as friends. I did not flat out say no to Sabrina or the other girls and neither did Shannon, but at lunch and recess we are usually busy playing sport to play with the girls and it was nothing personal. We still talk to them in class, and I even sat next to Sabrina Brewer for an entire year in assigned seats in grade 3 and we talked a bit.

Sabrina is pretty with blond hair, blue eyes and fair skin and just turned 12 years old in January and she is getting tall already and is pushing past 5'6 already and hit her growth spurt this year! I can tell and so can my friends. Sabrina does not play sport, but she is a competitive dancer and so are most of her friends.

The popular boys are complete idiots at school and worse than the girls! Especially those two idiots Peter and Sam and their friends Matt, Adam, and Jerry. Oh, trust me! Peter and Sam drive Shannon and I crazy and Robert and David. I have known those two boys since the start of primary school, and they are in the same class as us. Peter is cute looking with his red hair, green eyes and freckles and he is skinny and quite short. Shorter than me actually! Sam is very young-looking and is cute with his light brown hair and brown eyes and is also shorter than me! Robert and David too.
Peter and Sam did not like playing with girls until last year

and were always teasing Robert and David about playing with Shannon and I. So did Matt, Adam, and Jerry. Peter and Sam are immature and sexist and tease Robert and David a lot about playing with girls and are worse with Shannon and me! They are always teasing us.

So now that everyone is in grade six the children in the popular group play together and Sabrina is extremely popular, and the boys are starting to notice her, I think. Since she is pretty and popular.

I go to a public school, Jefferson primary school, the only primary school that is public in my town! The other primary school kids go to Liberty Grammar, which is grade prep to year 12 or to the next town to Rydall primary school or Ivory Grammar. The private school kids do not mix with the public-school kids though and it is the same with primary school and high school.
Most of my friends do not know any Liberty Grammar kids, since their school is far from us, but I unfortunately do! Since my dad is a lawyer and works for a firm that is run by Mr. and Mrs. Cummings and through my mum and dad sometimes, I am forced to mix with that complete snob Leanne Cummingo and her snobby older sister Marie. Since my dad works for their parents and my mum is a photographer and takes Leanne's photos, since she is a child model and occasionally does pageants too. Can you believe that? Leanne's family is wealthy, and Leanne and her sister are complete idiots.

Leanne Cummingo and I do not get along and sure do hate each other! It has been like that for years, since we were little, and my dad started working for her parents. Leanne is just too different to me and is very wealthy. She has a full-time babysitter, housekeeper, gardener, and chauffer working for her parents. All Leanne and I do is argue when we are together and she calls me all sorts of names, but I give it right back to her.

Leanne only plays with private school kids and her best friend is Allison Ritz from Liberty Grammar. I know Allison, although not too well. Just know her from seeing her with Leanne occasionally when I am forced to play with Leanne or go to functions that Leanne's parents organize. Allison and her parents are usually also invited. Allison is Japanese and has a twin brother Aaron. I hate Allison Ritz! She is as big a snob as Leanne and is always teasing my friends and I. Allison comes from a wealthy family too and lives in a mansion, has a babysitter, housekeeper, gardener, and chauffeur that work for her parents too.

So, I am quite happy with my friends, family and I like playing sport. I am happy with the way things are and am looking forward to my last year of primary school, although I am also nervous about starting high school too. It is going to be a big year!

Chapter 2

Stacey

On Friday I had a good day at school, although the work is getting harder now that we are in grade six. The teachers are dishing out more homework and school is getting more serious with preparing for high school next year. As my parents said, grade six is an important year for me and I need to start concentrating on my studies and not just sport, although they know how much I love sport and are proud of what I have achieved over the years with basketball and swimming.

I am not bad at school and don't mind reading. I like English as a subject and do well at it. I am not strong at maths or science and struggle with those. I'm also not good with music either, although music class at school can be fun. My passion is sport, definitely! I love sport and have been playing basketball since I was 7 years old and really love it. I am actually the girl's grade six basketball captain at school and spend a lot of time training and playing games. I am tall enough for basketball and love it and last year in grade five our team took out the grand finale against Rydal primary school in the public-school competition for rural schools. It's fun being on the school basketball team and because we are out in the country sometimes we take the bus out to other school's to play, which is fun, although our main competition is Rydal primary school. There are lots of primary schools in the competition though. I hope we can take the grand final again this year! We'll see. I also play basketball for a social team, which is fun and I have some great friends from basketball, especially my friend Anna. Anna goes to Rydal primary school and plays on their school team, but socially we are on the same basketball team and have been friends for years. I don't care what school she goes too! We are still very close and Anna is friends with Robert, David and Shannon too.

I don't just play basketball and have also been swimming for years, since I was about 3 years old! My parents had me in swimming lessons for me to be safe in our beach town and I took to swimming like a duck to water! I love it and have been swimming for years and now I am on the squad team at the local aquatic centre. I do races and swimming carnivals and also swim for the school team when we have swimming carnivals on.

I take swimming seriously and spend most of my time training, getting up early and doing races. I am very fast! I win most of my races and am a freestyle swimmer, short events. It's fun and I enjoy swimming as much as basketball, although having two sports I do takes up a lot of my time.

...

Enough on that though! On Friday spent the morning doing an English test that I hope I passed and handed in my homework and then we did some maths and it was time for recess. At recess I played with Shannon, Robert and David on the oval and at lunch too and we played soccer for most of lunch after we ate, which was fun.

That afternoon we had sports class and then the teacher did some more activities with us. My class is combined grade 5/6 this year and I have a good class and friends in class, which I am happy about. Shannon, Robert, and David are all in the same class as me. After school I stayed on with my friends. There was no training for basketball or swimming today. One of two days off for me! Monday and Friday from training or games and races, although I enjoy playing basketball and swimming and have no issues with all the training and games.

I went into after school care with my friends. Since my parents work full-time and I am not old enough to stay at home on my own. At least my parents said no! I think next year for year 7, I will be going home or to my grandparents' house after school, since there is no after-school care at Jefferson Secondary College.

It is ok though! I enjoy after school care and find it fun and do holiday programs every term and so do my friends. As grade six kids my friends and I usually do not need too much watching and even help a bit with the little grade preps and enjoy playing with them! It is fun and I like little kids.

After school care is fun, although it can be annoying having to be babysit still every afternoon, but my parents still prefer me to be looked after and not home on my own and my grandparents do not live close, more like a half an hour drive away.

I go to after school care every day after school and sometimes it is after basketball or swimming practice. I enjoy playing games and we always have something to eat and socializing with my friends is fun. Shannon, Robert, and David are all in after-school care too.

I also do holiday program and that is a lot of fun. We do heaps of excursions; movies and the workers take us out. We have nice childcare workers looking after us and a couple that we are close to and there are teenage helpers from high school helping too, that seem more like friends than workers. The teenagers are 15 years or older and all from Jefferson Secondary College. Gaining some work experience. They get paid to help and some used to go to after school care. They are not much older than my friends and I and I know a lot of Jefferson Secondary College kids and so do my friends of course. A lot of them are older brothers or sisters of my classmates and David's older brother goes to that school. So, when we visit David's house sometimes, he has his friends over.

That is my school next year and I am moving to the local high school and not Rydall Secondary College. Jefferson Secondary College is a lot more local and easier to get to too. Rydall Secondary is around a half an hour bus ride or car from our town and so is Rydall primary school.

Rydall primary school is our closest public school but to us and our main rivals for everything. From sport to academics and most of the time Jefferson kids do not have a good relationship with Rydall kids. My friend Anna goes there though and several friends from basketball after school. So, Robert, David Shannon and I have several friends from that school and Anna is especially close to our whole group.

I like kids and enjoy playing with the little grade preps and so do my friends. We all have buddies too in grade prep and I have a little girl that is my buddy and Angie loves playing with me. So that day I spent after school care playing with my friends and we had an afternoon snack and at around 5:30pm my mum picked me up and took me home, she works local and I am usually home by six and so are my friends. Their parents all work in town too. I said bye to my friends and headed home with my mum. I had dinner, watched some television with my parents and did some homework before I went to bed.

Chapter 3

Sabrina

Hi everyone, my name is Sabrina Brewer and I just turned 12 years old and am in grade six at Jefferson primary school. I come from a big family and live with my mum, dad and three sisters. I have two older sisters. Sandra, who is 17 years old and is in year 12 at Jefferson Secondary College and Monica, who is 15 years old and in year 10 at Jefferson Secondary College and my little sister, Alana. Who is the baby of the family and is 6 years old and is in grade 1 at my school. I am close to all my sisters and my parents too.

I have lots of friends at school and a few girls that I am particularly close with. Grace, Sophie, Elise, Amy, Emma, Vicky, and Charlotte are my closest friends, and we have all been friends since grade prep and are inseparable at school. I enjoy playing with my friends at school and outside school and we all enjoy playing together and I also have friends from dancing that I am close with outside school. Grace, Sophie, Amy, and Charlotte all dance too and I do ballet, jazz, tap, contemporary, lyrical and acrobatics. Dancing's my life! Trust me, I love it and often go to competitions and my team, and I usually win the competitions or place.

I used to play with just girls at school until the end of last year, when we started noticing boys! The boys used to drive us crazy in grade three and 4 and teased the girls and would not let us play with them. This year we usually play with the boys at lunch or watch them play sport though and a couple of boys we are close with. Matt, Adam and their friends Peter and Sam, but my main group at school is still girls and the boys are friends of ours, but not overly close and the girls still sometimes play on our own at lunch and recess if we want to practice dance routines and tricks, since most of my group dances or if we want to play on the playground when the boys are playing soccer or basketball, but sometimes we will play together, but only with the popular boys.

I am popular at school and have lots of friends, mostly girls, and I feel sorry for the girls that are not in the main group. Stacey Green or Shannon Chambers! I have nothing against Stacey or Shannon, and we play together sometimes after school and with their friend Robert, since we all live on the same street.

Being in grade six is good and we are the big kids at school! The little kids look up to us, although unless it is my little sister, I do not usually play with the grade ones and preps and Alana knows not to try and play with my group at lunch! She plays with the little kids, although if she has any problems, I will stick up for her and tell the kids off if I have too. Since that is what big sisters are for!

I do not really care about school and just like playing with my friends at school and do not really do well on the academic side of things. I prefer to dance or play with my friends.

I just got nominated for the female school captain though and am not sure if I will get it. There is always a male and female school captain from grade six to be fair. We will see! Depends on if I get voted for or not.

...

Enough on that though! So, on Friday after school my sister Monica picked Alana and I up and so did Sandy. Together, since they go to the same school. My parents prefer me to come home with my older sisters to be safe and I am not allowed to look after Alana on my own yet, although mum says in a couple of years, I will be able to.

That is ok though! I like it when Sandy and Monica pick me up from school. Since they are teenagers and Monica and I are close, since we are not far apart in age. I picked Alana up from her classroom and she came running up to give me a hug and I said to her, and I asked how her day was. I adore my little sister! Trust me. She is cute and has blond, curly hair, and blue eyes.

I walked out to the gates with Alana and said hi to Sandra and Monica. Sandra is great and we are close, although she is a lot older than me, and Sandra is often on babysitting duty! Since she is 17 years old and two years older than Monica, although she does not mind babysitting and spoils Alana rotten and adores her. Monica is 15 years old and babysits to help too. Sandra and I are also close and get along well and I look up to her.

I walked out with my sisters and Monica said to me that she is going up to The Avenue tonight and so is Sandra to hang out with some friends. She is talking lively about it with me, and I know that Monica enjoys Friday nights at The Avenue! I hear about it every week and Sandra goes too to spend time with her friends.

The Friday night teen party at The Avenue! My friends and I are all curious about it and older kids are always telling me how fun it is and that it is always full of teenagers from both Jefferson Secondary College and Liberty Grammar. I am always asking Monica about it! She knows that I am hankering to go and so do my friends. We are getting close to being teenagers anyway and will be in high school next year.

Monica is the cheekier teenager out of my two sisters. Sandra is more serious and takes school seriously and wants to go to university after school. She can be a lot of fun but and spends time with Alana and I and we have long talks.

Sandra has a group of friends at school, mainly a few close friends and they are all nice and often hang out at our place. Sandra also has a boyfriend, Michael, that she has been dating for a year, so that is another reason her group of friends is not that big. Michael is great. I really like him, and he met my parents and has a good relationship with Monica and I and adores little Alana. Michael helps Sandra babysit sometimes so they can spend time together and they go out too of course. Michael is like part of the family already. Sandra and Michaels group is the same and they are graduating high school this year. Both Sandra and Michael cannot wait to graduate and are talking about next year already.

Monica and I are closer in age. There is just a three-year age gap between us, and Monica seems more like a friend to me most of the time than an older sister. Monica and I are close but fight a lot. Monica's my biggest protector though, especially when we were both in primary school. I miss having Monica at school with me and now I just have my little sister Alana!

Monica was protective in primary school, and she is still protective of me and is a typical 15-year-old! Monica likes to hang out with her friends, talk to cute guys and go to parties and usually must get roped into babysitting on Friday or Saturday nights! Since I still need looking after and so does my little sister Alana. Monica does babysit though when Sandra is not available, and they rotate it. Monica and Sandra get along, but do not have the same group of friends at school. Monica is popular and has lots of friends and a guy that she likes. They are not officially dating, just seeing each other for now. Have been for a couple of months. My parents do not know about Monica's guy. Since they are not serious at 15 years old, and they have only seen each other for a couple of months.

Monica is popular and cheeky, and she parties a lot, has a lot of friends and likes to go out to the teen party at The Avenue, so does my older sister Sandra. It is a good chance for them to hang out with friends. I am almost a teenager anyway. I have one year to go before I turn 13 years old and have already developed early, and I know it. I am tall for my age, 5'6" tall and have breasts already and I got my period this year. Monica was one to explain what was happening! So was Sandra when I got my period and I talk to Monica a lot and she asks me if I have any crushes and so forth. What are big sisters for huh?

...

Anyway! So, as I was walking along with my sisters when Monica and Sandra asked if I wanted to go to the Avenue with them tonight. What? I gaped at them in disbelief. I am a bit too young for the teen party on Friday night, but sometimes grade six and year 7 kids go with their older brothers or sisters. Since there are a lot of teenagers there on a Friday night! So far, my parents have said a firm no to me though and said that I am too young, but what changed? Sandra said to me that my parents said that they want to go to the movies and dinner and Sandra offered to look after me tonight and Monica offered to help, since she gets to go to The Avenue I bet. Alana is going with my parents to dinner and the movie. Alana's way too young to go to The Avenue on Friday night. My parents would never allow it.

I was excited to go to The Avenue tonight with my older sisters and asked Sandra if I could invite a couple of friends. I am assuming Sandra is in charge tonight. My parents trust her more than Monica with me. Monica can be a bit irresponsible, my mum said. Especially when she is with her friends!
Sandra said OK, but only two friends and I decided to invite Grace and Sophie. They do not live far from me, and I knew that their mum would allow it if Sandra were there. Sandra is 17 years old and very responsible and does not mind looking after us kids! That is one of the things I like about Sandra. She has no issues babysitting and says that she enjoys it and likes my friends and me.

So, we walked home and were all hanging out at my house and Sandra studied for a bit before we went out for an hour or so. She is in year 12 and has a lot of homework every night. I am not looking forward to that! Neither is my sister Monica. So, Monica oversees Alana while Sandra studies and we were both playing with Alana and having fun with her and I talked to Monica too, we are awfully close. We had something to eat too. Just a snack. I will be having dinner at The Avenue tonight and so will Monica and Sandra.

My parents got back at 5:30pm and said hi to us and by then it was time for my first night out at The Avenue teen party, although it won't be a late night. I'm just there for dinner and Sandra will bring me home after that. Monica said she might kick on at The Avenue after that and is more into the then Sandra is. There is a Disk jockey after 9:30pm and my mum said I'm not allowed to stay for that. Since I am too young. Grade six and year 7 kids usually just go for dinner part and don't stay for the Disk jockey, although it's exciting to go just for dinner.

Michael is coming to the Avenue with us and helping Sandra look after Grace, Sophie and I. We are all going to dinner at The Avenue. Monica agreed to come with us and help babysit but wants to spend time with her friends too.

I rung Grace and Sophie and they got permission from their parents to come to The Avenue tonight and my parents were also ok with that. I went upstairs to get ready and put on a denim skirt, a t-shirt and had some nice sandals and I left my blond hair out and did not put makeup on, since I am not allowed to wear it yet. Mum said next year when I am in high school, although I am allowed to shave my legs and wear jewelry. So, I put on a bracelet and a necklace and was feeling excited. This is my first time at a teen party at The Avenue. Which is a weekly event that is approved of by all the adults in town. Parents like knowing where their kids are and that they are at a supervised party. It is an underage party with no drinking allowed or fights or smoking. I know when I am in high school my friends and I will be there every week. As it is really the main teen party in town. I am looking forward to going tonight.

I went downstairs and hung out with Monica and Sandra a bit, we are waiting for Grace and Sophie to be dropped off. I was having fun though and looking forward to my night out.

Chapter 4

Sabrina

By 7:00pm I was heading to The Avenue with my sisters. We walked up there. Since it is close and I was with Sandra, Monica, Sandra's guy Michael, plus Grace and Sophie. I like Michael. He is very friendly and has a good relationship with my whole family. Monica is meeting some friends at The Avenue and Monica is looking forward to seeing Dan, who is the guy she likes and is seeing.

It was not a long walk and Sandra told Grace, Sophie, and I to walk with her and Michael and not get lost. She is always like that! Especially if we go out, but she is just being responsible and I still adore Sandra, we are awfully close. I was having fun with Grace and Sophie, and we are close friends. I have known them since grade prep, and we are still close. Grace and Sophie are fraternal twins.

Once we got to The Avenue Sandra and Michael organized a picnic table for us and were talking about going to get us dinner. The local pizza place has discounted pizza for the teen night and my parents gave Sandra and Monica money to get dinner, snacks, and drinks.

Sandra and Michael were really the ones looking after us! Monica is already off talking to friends and Dan, although she was not kissing him. Sandra would kill her if she did that in front of my friends and I. Sandra and Michael were not kissing or anything, just hanging out and talking and a couple of their friends came over to say hi and asked who the kids are about Grace, Sophie and I and said that we are cute. I like Sandra's friends and they were friendly and quite happy to join our picnic table and talked to Grace, Sophie and I and did not leave us out and neither did Sandra and Michael. Although they are a lot older than us! Year 12 students and all at least 17 years old. I liked hanging out with the big kids! So did Grace and Sophie.

Monica was there with her friends and Dan, the guy she likes. Dan came and said hello too, but their group made their own picnic table next to us. It was a large group. I am having fun! My sisters made sure not to leave us out and were talking to us and hanging out.

More groups were coming into The Avenue by then and Sandra and Michael went up to get some pizza, leaving Monica in charge of Grace, Sophie, and me. So, we sat at her table for a bit and talked to her friends. I got off the table a bit and so did Grace and Sophie, we wanted to sit on the brick wall facing the beach while we waited. Monica was annoyed at that! Although she took us. She is babysitting while Sandra is gone and wanted to spend time with her friends, and I can tell that she is a bit annoyed! Monica is talking to us though and asking if we are having fun and I was enjoying my first night at The Avenue and hanging out with the big kids.

Monica tensed up a bit when a black limousine pulled up at The Avenue and so did a few of her friends. What was that about? I was surprised to see the limousine and so were Grace and Sophie. Who around here travels in limousines? Monica's friend Alice came up to Monica and so did Dan and they looked annoyed and said to Monica.

"Great it's got to be the Liberty Grammar girls."
Oh, that is who it was! I know about Liberty Grammar. It is the local private school in town that goes from grade prep to year 12. I do not know any kids from there and neither do my friends. Since us public primary school kids do not mix with the private school kids and rarely come to The Avenue and stick to our own friends.

I know from my sister Monica that the Liberty Grammar girls in her year level are complete idiots and Monica is always backstabbing them! Calling them complete snobs.

Sandra sticks away from the drama, although she does not like Liberty Grammar kids either, but there is not much trouble with the year 12 kids between Jefferson Secondary College and Liberty Grammar. Monica's year 10 class however!
I was still there with Monica and Sandra and Michael were not back yet, they were still up at The Avenue getting dinner and trusted Monica with us and her friends. Since they are 15 years old and some of Sandra's friends are at the other table, although I do not know! My parents do not let me go to The Avenue just with Monica and only if Sandra is there. It is because Monica can be irresponsible and likes to hang out with her friends and boyfriends, but

she is a good person and I adore my older sister and get along very well with Monica, like I do with Sandra.

The limousines pulled up in front of The Avenue and Monica and Alice rolled their eyes and said that it is those Liberty Grammar snobs and were ignoring me and Grace and Sophie, although Monica told me to stay on the brick wall and not try to approach the Liberty Grammar kids. Monica is protective of me and knows that I am just a kid and in primary school Monica often stuck up for me when she was in grade six and I was a little grade three kid. Sometimes getting into arguments and threatening older girls that were trying to pick on my friends or I and nothing is changed! Monica's still protective of me.
I watched the limousine pull up and so did Grace and Sophie and we talked and said that the limousine is cool, but you had to be from the rich side of town to afford one of those. Gresham Avenue is where all the rich kids live and go to school and the beachside properties.

Monica and her friends tensed immediately and out of the limousines came 4 or five girls, including kids! I was surprised. There were two girls that are Monica's age I think and another two that look like they are 11 or 12 years old and clearly, they are here with their older sisters or cousins like I am tonight.

Monica said to Alice.

"Great it's Marie Cummingo and Lara Ritz from Liberty Grammar."

They are the older ones, but Monica also commented.

"What are Allison Ritz and Leanne Cummingo doing here? They are just in grade six at Liberty Grammar. Marie and Lara must be babysitting like us."

Allison and Leanne huh! I have never heard those two names in my life, although clearly, they are my age and Grace and Sophies too and we are in the same grade, although at different schools.
I asked Monica who they are, and Monica said that Marie is in year 10 at Liberty Grammar and is Leanne's older sister and Lara Ritz is the older cousin of Allison, who is also in year 10 at Liberty Grammar. Monica said to me quickly that she hates Marie and Lara, and they are always making trouble for my sister Monica and teases Sandra sometimes, although they are brave to do that, when Sandra is older than them.

I was glad to see some grade six kids at The Avenue! Although annoyed that they are from Liberty Grammar. I feel swamped by teenagers tonight, although I am having fun.

Marie and Lara paid the driver and walked into The Avenue with Allison and Leanne and Marie spotted my sister quickly and gave Monica a dirty look and Monica's friend Monica returned it and so did her friends. Particularly Alice, who is Monica's best friend. They do everything together and Alice is a regular at my house. Alice quickly joined Monica and shot daggers at Marie and Lara too.

Oh no! I am starting to understand why my parents do not trust Monica to babysit me on her own at The Avenue. There is always trouble on Friday night, especially with the Liberty Grammar girls. Marie came up to Monica and had Lara, Allison and Leanne with her and Marie teased Monica and said that her outfit looks like it comes from a bargain basement shop.

What? Who does Marie think she is talking to my sister Monica like that? Who is this witch? I was angry on Monica's behalf, although I would not start trouble with teenagers and trust me! Monica can handle herself and called Marie a snob and that she had better leave her alone if she knew what was good for her.

Monica and Marie got into an argument after that, right in front of us kids, although I do not blame Monica and am angry with the Liberty Grammar girls' comments too. Lara joined in too and argued with Alice. Oh boy!
The teenagers were still arguing when suddenly Allison Ritz and Leanne Cummingo noticed me and my friends Grace and Sophie sitting on the brick wall. Great! They are my age and in grade six and Leanne's sister is a complete idiot that is calling my older sister names and is currently in an argument with her and Allison's older cousin Lara is no better.

Allison came over to the brick wall straight away and she sure is confident! So am I though, and I hated Allison on sight and am surprised to see that she is Asian and so is her older cousin Lara. We don't have any Asian girls at my school, although it doesn't matter and I think that Allison is pretty and has great hair with her black hair, almond shaped eyes and she is well dressed and I would have told her that and tried to be friendly and so would Grace and Sophie, if our sisters and cousins hadn't of started an argument.

Allison's friend Leanne is also good-looking and looks older than grade six and is very tall! She is my height, whereas Allison is short. Leanne has brown hair, brown eyes, and olive skin.

Allison came over to the bench and introduced herself to me and Grace and Sophie by calling me a bimbo! Not saying hi of course. What did Allison just call me? I don't even know her and she's already insulting me. I know that Allison's annoyed by my sister's comments to her cousin and Leanne's sisters, which is why she's calling me names, but that was low!

Allison came over to the bench and introduced herself to me and Grace and Sophie by calling me a bimbo! Not saying hi of course. What did Allison just call me? I don't even know her and she's already insulting me. I know that Allison's annoyed by my sister's comments to her cousin and Leanne's sisters, which is why she's calling me names, but that was low!

I'm no wallflower myself though and am keen to prove to Monica that I'm not scared of these Liberty Grammar girls either and called Allison a b... for calling me a bimbo and we got into our first argument! A bad one and Allison was calling me names and Grace and Sophie too and Leanne joined in to and was just as bad as Allison and was calling me names and said that I'm a bimbo too.

So now us kids were arguing as much as Monica was with Marie and Lara and Alice and Allison sure is a goer! Wow. She doesn't hold back in an argument and neither does Leanne and I was just as bad. Marie wasn't taking notice of us and was busy arguing herself, but I was starting to get pissed! Who are these idiots Allison and Leanne? Clearly they have a problem with me and my friends Grace and Sophie for absolutely no reason!

My argument with Allison was interrupted when Sandra came back with Michael and they had some pizza boxes and drinks, which they put on the table and Sandra looked very pissed! At me and also Monica and came over to the group and exclaimed.

"What the hell is going on?"

Monica looked embarrassed and stopped arguing with Marie and Marie rounded up her little sister too and so did Lara with her cousin Allison. Clearly when the big kids get back, they can help stop the trouble! Sandra and Michael are in year 12 and so are their friends that helped get the food and they came and broke up the argument. Mine with Allison and Leanne. We were still arguing when Sandra arrived. Sandra told me to stop it and that she would tell my parents if I did not stop trying to make trouble and warned Leanne and Allison to stop arguing too and leave me alone. Grace and Sophie had not gotten involved in the argument and left me to it, although they were standing with me. Grace and Sophie are the least likely of my school friends to start trouble with the Liberty Grammar girls and they are the quietest of the group. If Elise, Vicky, or Charlotte were there they would have been arguing too. Grace and Sophie are just like that though and I do not hold it against them. They are two of my best friends and I am protective of them.

Leanne Cumingo sure is not like Grace and Sophie! Leanne is clearly as loud, argumentative, and happy to insult as Allison Ritz is. Allison is a shocker, and I could not stand Allison or Leanne in sight and when my sister Sandra arrived, I was in the middle of a screaming match with Allison and Leanne. The other teenagers at The Avenue looked amused actually and Marie and Lana looked annoyed. They were not expecting Allison and Leanne to join in the argument and now us kids were worse than our older sisters and cousins. Monica looked amused actually and not as annoyed with me as Sandra is. In fact, Monica looked proud and said that when we got home later that she could see that I took after her and she was proud of the way I handled myself and so was Alice. Monica did not dare say that to Sandra but. Only to me later.

Sandra does not look proud of me and in fact she is furious and got me away from Allison and Leanne quickly and Grace and Sophie and warned Monica to leave the Liberty Grammar kids alone too. Monica knows she has to listen to Sandra too or she will be in trouble with my parents. Sandra told me to sit at her picnic table and Michael was there too and their other friends. Michael was shocked by the argument too, but stayed out of it. Sandra sat next to Monica on our table and said that they need to talk. Monica sat down and had something to eat at our table for now, but she is still itching to go back to her friends and Dan, I can tell.

Marie and Lara went and sat at another table with Allison

and Leanne and those two idiots still give me dirty looks! I am not scared of them though. Monica was sitting next to Sandra and Dan came and sat next to her on the other side and Alice, their other friends, were at the table next to us. We made one large group and ate pizza and garlic bread, with soft drinks and I was having fun and talking to everyone, and dinner was delicious.

Sandra and Monica were sitting next to each other on purpose, or Monica Dan and Alice would still be on the other table. Sandra wanted to talk to Monica before she disappeared with her friends and boyfriend and takes her role as older sister to me and Monica seriously. Sandra is strict when she babysits me, although she is a lot of fun too and I cannot imagine Sandra starting trouble with the Liberty Grammar kids like Monica did tonight. Monica and Marie were about one step away from a fight and I know it.

Monica has been in physical fights before and I know that she has hit Marie before after an argument went too far earlier this year. Monica told me all about the fight. My sister does not shy away from punching on and in fact is happy to hit someone that is messing around with her friends. Monica has taught me to fight too, and I can handle myself in a punch on if I must, although so far no one has hit me yet. I do not know but! Allison and Leanne pushed me far tonight. I like to think that they would not start a physical fight, but if they ever did I would not back away from one. My parents were furious at the fight between Monica and Marie and grounded my sister after that. Monica and Marie hate each other, it has been like that since the start of high school.

That is why there was trouble tonight. Sandra is not happy with Monica or me, but especially Monica and got into a disagreement with my sister and said that she was being ridiculous and irresponsible and what was with that stupid argument with the Liberty Grammar girls. Monica explained what happened to Sandra and said she did not start the argument and I backed her up and so did Alice and told Sandra how Marie just marched right up to Monica and started insulting her and so did Lara and Monica was not going to back away from an argument and Allison and Leanne started on me. Sandra got annoyed at the Liberty Grammar girls after that and called them idiots and not worth it. She is not happy about the argument, but understands and hates the Liberty Grammar kids too, she was worried about me and reminded Monica that I am only 12 years and she left her in charge of me and Monica was arguing right in front of me and being a bad influence. Sandra is not happy with Monica, but also is not happy with me and said that she is not going to take me to The Avenue again if I act like that again, but she can tell that Allison and Leanne are brats and I need to stay away from them. Sandra stopped after that and we had some fun.

I stayed at The Avenue with my sisters and their friends and left after a while and Sandra and Michael took me home. Monica's going to stay for the disc jockey and party with her friends a bit. She will not be back late, but dad picks her up at The Avenue to make sure she is safe coming home.

We dropped Grace and Sophie off and when I got home mum and dad were there and Sandra and Michael headed out on their own. Saying they might just spend time together at Michael's parents' house a bit. My parents are fine with that. I went up to my room and thought about that night and am still a bit shaken up by my argument with Allison Ritz and Leanne Cummingo. Those stupid b...! I do not like them, and they do not like me clearly. I am not sure, but I do not think that this will be my only argument with that witch Allison Ritz or her friend Leanne Cummingo.

Chapter 5

Stacey

On Monday at school Sabrina Brewer was sitting with her friends Grace and Sophie in class and had Elise with her. I was sitting next to Shannon and Robert at the next table and David was there too. Sabrina was in a fine mood that day and I was amused. She was talking about Friday night with her friends and the teacher had not arrived yet. So, we were all just talking. I said hi to Sabrina, Elise, Grace, and Sophie. We are on speaking, terms, but do not play together too much at school although Sabrina is friends with Robert, Shannon, David, and me.

Sabrina sat with the girls but and was talking about Friday night at The Avenue and said that she went to the teen party with her older sisters Sandra and Monica. What is Sabrina doing at the teen party? Same with Grace and Sophie that went with her. That is for the high school kids, although grade six kids sometimes go for dinner and that is it if they are with older siblings or cousins.

I do not go and neither do my friends yet, we are too young, and I do not have older siblings, although I am curious about it and so are my friends. Sabrina said that dinner was fun, but that the Liberty Grammar girls ruined it for her and that she got into an argument with Allison Ritz and Leanne Cummingo from Liberty Grammar and Sabrina was saying that she hates Allison and Leanne already and said that they look like complete snobs like Marie and Lara that were with them.

How does Sabrina know Leanne Cummingo? I was very curious. I know Leanne Cummingo through my parents. My dad works for Leanne's parents as a solicitor and my mum is a photographer and my mum sometimes does Leanne's professional photos.

So, I know Leanne! Also, her older sister Marie and Leanne's mum and dad. I hate Leanne Cummingo though and think that she is a complete snob. Leanne is a child model and often does beauty pageants too. Which is why my mum often takes her professional photos.

Leanne and I do not get along and that is an understatement! Our parents often force us in together for play dates and we get mixed in for functions. All we ever do is argue and Leanne is always teasing me, although if she is forced to play with me and her mum is there, she will leave me alone, but I hate that witch! Also, her older sister Marie.

. . .

So, Sabrina was having a good backstab of Allison and Leanne while we waited for the teacher to come in. I do not blame her and think that Allison Ritz and Leanne Cummingo are idiots too. I know Allison Ritz too. How can I not? Allison is Leanne's best friend, and they are awfully close. Allison's sometimes at those stupid functions that I am forced to go to with my parents too, but not all the time. Allison is also always teasing me and calling me names when we see each other.

I tuned back to Sabrina and said that I hate Leanne and Allison too and she asked how I know them. Sabrina and I are not that close friends, but we talk in class, and she does with Shannon and Robert too and we have occasionally played together after school too. Sabrina asked how I know Allison and Leanne and I told her, and both agreed that they are idiots and so did Robert and Shannon and Sabrina's friends too.

…

Once the teacher walked in, we stopped talking and did some work and I was relieved when recess came around and then lunch. I had fun with Robert, David and Shannon and we spent lunch playing soccer and talking.

After school that day I had swimming practice for an hour before after school care. I do swimming training on Monday afternoons and Wednesday afternoons and basketball training is usually on Tuesday afternoons. Leaving only Thursday and Friday afternoons off for me. I usually have basketball games on Saturday afternoon and go to the school swimming carnivals too when they are on.

I only swim for the school team and no longer at the local pool. It is a bit too much being on two swimming teams. I used to play basketball at school and for a social team and swim at the pool and at school until this year. That is just my parents! Trust me. I spent most of my time playing sport and love it, but my grades at school were slipping a bit, so mum and dad agreed to me being on the school teams for swimming and basketball and the basketball team at school keeps me busy and so does swimming.

We walked up to the swimming school and then I walked in and got changed and was in a one-piece bathing suit. Ava our after-school care worker dropped us off that are in swimming lessons, made sure we all got to our classes and then we were ready to go!

Chapter 6

Stacey

By the time that Ava left me to my class I had said hi to my instructor and friends in the class. Which is mixed from kids from my school and kids that are from year 7 and 8 at Jefferson Secondary College. I am one of the youngest on the advanced swim team and you can join squad from grade six for the school team. They mix grade six kids with year 7 and 8 because it is an advanced squad, and you must have been swimming since the start of primary school or earlier. Like I have. I started swimming at 3 years old!

It is considered an honour to get on the swim team at school and you must take tests and pass all the other swimming levels to make squad. I have been doing squad all year now and enjoy it. It is a lot of fun and I enjoy going to swimming carnivals and competing against other schools.

I said hi to my friends on the team and there are two more grade six girls on the team and two boys, and the rest of the kids are from year 7 and 8. About 12 of us in total and

I like hanging out with the big kids! So do my friends, although they are not too much older than us. I like hearing about Jefferson Secondary College and hearing all the gossip! It is fun. I will be at that school anyway next year and my parents said that and asked if I want to go to Jefferson Secondary College or out to Rydal Secondary College, which is also not far, but in another town. I prefer to go to the local high school though and so do Robert, Shannon, and David.

The instructor came out and said hi to everyone and we all got in the pool. I had on my favourite bathers. My blue ones, goggles and my hair tucked into a cap.
I have been swimming for years now and really love it. I am a good swimmer and enjoy freestyle particularly and am good at the shorter events.

Swim Squad training on Monday nights go for an hour and an hour on Wednesday night. That is for the school team, and I am only doing that now. After school swimming and on weekends have early morning trainings too, but my parents want me to focus on one sport after school. So, I am just playing basketball after school. The older high school kids have their own swim team and at Jefferson Secondary it is a very popular and competitive sport. They train a lot more at the age. Every day.

The coach started us off with some stroke training and techniques and we were working on some freestyle training. My favourite! Then we swam some laps. A pair at a time and my opponent was my friend Alexa. Who is in year 7 at Jefferson Secondary College. She is a great swimmer and my main competition on the team. Although in school sports, we compete against other schools too.

The coach usually gets the girls to swim against each other and boys to swim against each other to see where we are at and shaping up against the competition! It is not the coach being sexist. At swim meets I will be competing against other girls and usually win a lot of races, although Alexa does too! We have gone first and second a few times in freestyle.

I won this round! Getting Alexa by half a head! I was happy, it's not a serious competition between us. We're friends, although we are competitive and so is everyone else on the team. After I had my race with Alexa we spent some more time in the pool, watching the other kids race and we were working on more strokes.

Swimming was over after an hour or so and I was thoroughly stuffed! The coach worked us hard, like the always do, but it's paying off and we have a meet coming up. A swimming carnival in a few weeks.

I went to the change room, had a shower and then got changed into some jeans and a t-shirt. I pulled my blond hair back into a ponytail. I was heading back to after school care Ava was waiting outside and is walking back and we didn't wait too long. I headed back with Ava and my two friends. Glad with how swimming had gone.

Chapter 7

Leanne

After school on Friday, I was spending some time with my older sister Marie, and we were watching television. It has been a long day and week and I am looking forward to spending some time relaxing.

Anyway! So hi, my name is Leanne Cummingo and I just turned 12 years old and am in grade six at Liberty Grammar in Queensland. I live with my parents and my older sister Marie, who is in year 10 at Liberty Grammar. We are a wealthy family and live on Gresham Avenue and my parents are both wealthy and work hard and after school my nannie is officially in charge of me since I am only 12 years old. There is a full-time babysitter/housekeeper at the house, a gardener and chauffer for my parents and we live in a mansion on Gresham Avenue. It is double story, with 4 bedrooms, 3 bathrooms, study, theatre room, retreat area, a large kitchen and study and the backyard is big, with a pool and tennis courts.

I have a good relationship with my parents and older sister and like my school Liberty Grammar and it is the only private school in town and the only real choice for my sister and I to go to school, unless we want to go to Jefferson Secondary primary or Secondary school or travel to the next town to go to Ivory Grammar. There is no way I would ever want to go to Jefferson primary or Secondary school! Neither would my older sister Marie. Are you kidding? With those public-school idiots that go to those schools!

I do not have a good relationship with public school kids and have never had a good relationship with them or had friends from Jefferson primary school or Rydall primary school. My friends and I also do not have a good relationship with kids from Ivory Grammar, although that school is remarkably like Liberty Grammar. Our schools are too competitive with each other and there is a lot of rivalry between the schools. All my friends are from Liberty Grammar.

The situation with Jefferson primary school this year is getting worse between us grade six kids. I am starting to understand what my sister Marie is talking about when she says the Jefferson Secondary kids are trouble and now my friend Allison and I completely agree. We are starting to hate Jefferson primary school kids.

I know several kids from Jefferson primary school, although I do not have a good relationship with any of them. I know Stacey Green, who is the same age as me and in grade six too at her school. Stacey and I have known each other for a few years since her dad started working for my parents.

I do not like Stacey Green and neither does my sister Marie. Stacey and I are just too different and all we ever do is argue and my parents are constantly forcing me to go to Stacey's house when my mum wants to visit Stacey's mum. My mum is good friends with Stacey Greens mum and our dads are friends too.

Whenever I see Stacey and go to her house or she comes to mine, we usually end up in an argument. My mum must drag me over to visit and Stacey hates being forced to play with me too. We just do not get along!

Whenever I see Stacey and go to her house or she comes to mine, we usually end up in an argument. My mum must drag me over to visit and Stacey hates being forced to play with me too. We just do not get along!

Stacey's friends Shannon, Robert and David are not any better and I still cannot believe Stacey's best friend is Robert and she is close to David too. Boys huh! Stacey's a big active child and so is Shannon Chambers though and I know Shannon Robert and David because they are often at the beach or playground, we all go to, or the kids play centre. There are only so many places for primary school kids to go to in town.

I do not have a good relationship with Shannon either and she is fiery! As much as Stacey is and is always arguing with me. Enough on that though! I do not really want to think about Stacey Green or her friends.

My best friend at school is Allison Ritz, who lives across the road son's family is hugely wealthy and lives in the biggest mansion on Gresham Avenue. Allison is great and we come from similar backgrounds. Allison is very wealthy and so is her family and Allison and I live across the road from each other. So, I have grown up going to Allison's house and she to mine and I love her whole family and Allison is close to me and my older sister Marie and my parents too.

Allison and I are popular at Liberty Grammar and have lots of friends and Allison's twin brother Aaron is good friends with me too. Allison and Aaron are close. Allison can be bossy in our group at school though and is our unannounced leader of the popular group and decides who is in and out of the group and both of us tease the less popular kids we do not like.

I have a good group at school and like my friends and my sister Marie is in year 10 and is extremely popular too at school and it is cool having an older sister and my friends think that it is cool too and like Marie and Marie and I get along well, and she does not me leave out when she is around her friends.

Marie passed onto me the hating of the Jefferson primary and Secondary College kids and I have been hearing about all the trouble for years from Marie and that Marie hates Monica from Jefferson Secondary College and Alice. I have been listening to this for years and I do not like Stacey Green from Jefferson primary school, but do not know any other kids too well from that school. Until last Friday night! Wow. I was at The Avenue for the first time with Marie, Allison Ritz, and her older cousin Lara. Allison and I have been asking for months to go to The Avenue on Friday night to the teen party, but my mum said not unless I am with Marie. Since I am incredibly young to be going and Marie agreed to look after me Friday night and so did Allison's older cousin Lara.

I found it fun going to dinner on The Avenue and was the first time I have been there. Marie was good about not leaving me out, although the night started out bad with that argument that Marie got into with Monica from Jefferson Secondary College.

Monica is an idiot and got into a loud argument with my sister and so did Allison's cousin Lara with Monica's friend Alice in front of us kids, although Allison and I found that amusing and know that if my parents knew then they would not be happy with Marie, but I will not tell them! I thought those girls are idiots too.

Monica was there with her younger sister, who was at The Avenue with her older sister like I was, and I quickly spotted Sabrina and her two friends Grace and Sophie. Allison and I were not happy with the argument between my sister and Lara and Sabrina's sister and Alice. Allison is feisty and tough and not shy about getting into arguments at school and most of the girls in our class fear Allison and me. As we are extremely popular.

Sabrina looked innocent sitting on the bench with her friends, although annoyed at the argument. Sabrina is tall and has blond hair, blue eyes and she is very skinny. She looked harmless and Allison and I have never heard of Sabrina Brewer, surprisingly. She goes to a different school to us, lives in a different neighbourhood and does not mix with our school. Sabrina is good looking actually and so is her older sister Marie. Allison said that to me privately later when we discussed it, but I would never tell her that! Give her satisfaction.

Allison was not particularly looking for trouble when she called Sabrina a bimbo. Allison did that for fun and she was annoyed at the argument and thought that Sabrina would fear her due to our reputation in the neighbourhood with the public-school kids.

Boy was Allison ever wrong! So was I and this innocent looking blond, blue eyed 12-year-old suddenly got up off the bench and started arguing back to Allison loudly and calling her names. Allison and Sabrina quickly got into a loud argument that half of The Avenue could hear.

Allison was shocked to say the least and so was I. To stand up to Allison Ritz like that and me is brave and who is this witch? Sabrina is clearly tough and has no issues getting into arguments and Allison picked the wrong girl to call a bimbo. I was even a bit amused, although I would not tell Allison that. Sabrina obviously does not like kids from our school and called Allison a snob quickly.

I was a bit worried about how far this argument was going to go and wondering if Allison is going to hit Sabrina or the other way around. If that happened, I know that Allison would fight back and that I would be forced to back her up and hit someone too. Sabrina's friends on the bench. I can fight, but I do not hit anyone unless they start it, or Allison gets hit.

Monica was there with her younger sister, who was at The Avenue and Allison, and I quickly spotted Sabrina and her two friends Grace and Sophie. We were not happy with the argument between my sister and Sabrina's sister and Sabrina looked harmless! With her blond hair and blue eyes and she is very skinny and pretty, although we would not tell her that.

Allison though it would be fun to tease Sabrina and called her a bimbo and we were just annoyed at the argument that was going on and to both our surprises Sabrina Brewer gave it right back to Allison and called her names and they got into an argument! A loud one and Sabrina was also calling me names.

Wow! Who is this witch? Allison and I were wondering quickly. Clearly Sabrina has no issues getting into arguments and does not like girls from our school and

Sabrina's brave to argue with Allison and I like that! It was even amusing. The girls at my school are all weary of Allison Ritz and I and know that we can fight. (Fist fights. I am not shy about getting into fights).

Allison did not back down though and got into a big argument with Sabrina, as bad as Monica's with Marie and Lara's with Alice and the argument got broken up by Sabrina's other older sister Sandra, who is in year 12 and 17 years old. So that is how we got introduced to Sabrina! Grace and Sophie too, although they were quiet and did not get into an argument with us.

We avoided those girls the rest of the night and just had dinner at The Avenue, but Allison rang me the next day and had a big talk to me about Sabrina Brewer and said that she thinks that Sabrina is a complete b… and had no right to get into an argument with Allison like that at The Avenue and me too. Allison asked around after that and talked to her cousin Lara and I talked to Marie, and we also asked around about Sabrina Brewer. Marie told me to watch out for Sabrina Brewer. She knows all about her from her older sister Monica. Marie said that Sabrina is turning into a grade six version of her sister Monica and is trouble for us Liberty Grammar kids if that is the case. Sabrina's whole family are proud to be middle class and go to public school. I know all about Monica from my sister Marie of course and Lara.

At Jefferson Secondary College Marie and Alice are extremely popular and head the popular group in year 10. Sandra, the oldest sister, is not a troublemaker and stays away from the drama. Monica's a different story and she is trouble and got into a fight with my sister earlier this year and Monica hates all of us Liberty Grammar girls. Marie said to me seriously that Sabrina is heading in the same direction as her sister and in high school Monica is likely to be protective of her little sister.

Sabrina is in trouble on her own without the help of her sister. I think and so does Allison. Allison's heard that Sabrina's the most popular girl in grade six at Jefferson primary school and has a large group of friends. From what we have heard Sabrina is the unannounced leader of her friends at school and is also popular with the boys and there are boys in the group too.

Sabrina Brewer is the public-school version of Allison Ritz and Allison and I both know it. She is good looking, popular, happy to get into arguments, teases the less popular girls and has an older sister that will help her out in high school next year and will mentor her too, like Marie and Lara will help Allison and I next year. Sabrina's trouble and likely to be competition for Allison and me in high school and we both know it.

As much as I hate Stacey Green and her friends Shannon, Robert, and David. I know that she is not trouble like Sabrina Brewer is. Stacey's harmless and does not have many friends and to be honest she fears Allison and I and our friends, or I would like to think so. Although Stacey can get pretty fired up with me and we get into a lot of arguments. Stacey does not have a lot of friends but is not likely to cause major trouble for the Liberty Grammar girls. Shannon is also quiet and rarely causes trouble for us.

Although I cannot stand Stacey, Shannon, Robert, or David.

Sabrina Brewer is different, and I was even shocked at the argument at The Avenue the other night. I was even amused at the argument between Allison and Sabrina, although I would not tell them that. They sure did go for it after meeting each other for like five minutes. Allison and Sabrina hated each other at sight. I do not like Sabrina either and think that she is an idiot and do not appreciate all the nasty comments the other night. Sabrina had better not mess with me or Allison again or there will be trouble, and Allison said that. I do not think this will be the first run in we have with her, and I have heard that Sabrina's friends are not any better, particularly Emma, Vicky and Charlotte are feisty too. It should be interesting to see what happens.

…

Anyway! So that night I just spent some time with Marie. We are very close and Marie is protective of me. We watched a movie and talked and then I went upstairs to my room, read a magazine and just spent some time on my own. Screw those Jefferson primary school girls! I thought as I hung out.

Chapter 8

Stacey

On Friday after school a week later I was looking forward to a weekend of relaxing and not doing much. It has been a long week and I have a basketball match tomorrow, that I am looking forward to. On Friday Shannon, Robert and David came over to my place. We got picked up by my mum at after school care and she does not mind having my friends over. My mum really loves Shannon and Robert and watched them grow up with me. They are like family with her and mum loves David too and thinks that he is a great kid.

After my mum picked us up and drove us back to my place mum got us something to eat and then we put a movie on in the lounge. We were waiting for my dad and then mum said that we would have some pizza for dinner. My mum does not mind looking after us and offered! Shannon's parents are busy working and so are Robert's. They own a shop and work late sometimes on Friday nights and David wanted to come over too.

Mum's officially babysitting, although I do not like it when she calls it that! I am in grade six now and do not need a lot of looking after, but mum prefers it if I do not stay at home on my own still, especially at night. I was having fun with my friends and the movie we put on is a comedy that we all enjoyed, and we ate too many snacks during it and talked. My dad came home while the movie was just finishing and said hi to Robert, Shannon and David and had the pizzas with him. Mum told him to pick it up on the way home. The pizza was yum and my parents are being good hosts tonight and are having fun with us and my mum asked my friends how their parents are, and we ate pizza and had some soft drinks.

After dinner I retreated down to the game room with my friends to give my parents a break and just because we wanted to. My parents have a well-set up game room downstairs, that I use and my friends, although my parents sometimes enjoy playing games too with me and I ask them to play with me if my friends are not around.

The game room is fun, and we have a billiards table, air hockey table and a television in the room with a comfortable couch and a coffee table with it and there is a games console attached to the television and blu ray player. I love playing video games! So do my friends. We have a couple of favorite games that we can play all day and if I am on a game too long my parents will come downstairs and tell me to do something else, but I usually get a good amount of game time.

We like air hockey and billiards too but were not in the mood for that after pizza for dinner. I turned the television on and put on of our favorite games, which was a fighting game, and we did our usual method when there are four players. Two played, then the winner played someone else until they lost. It is fun. My friends and I can do this all day! Trust me and I beat Robert and then Shannon, but David got me and challenged Robert.

I talked to my friends as we were playing video games and Shannon commented to me.

"What was going on with Sabrina now? When she was backstabbing Allison and Leanne. I did not even think she knows them."

Shannon and I talked about it a bit and yes, we have all heard about the famous argument at The Avenue between Sabrina and Allison! The whole school knows it by now, at least our class does and it is amusing. Sabrina has spent the whole week calling Allison Ritz and Leanne Cummingo every name in the sun.

Must have been some argument! I have never heard Sabrina Brewer backstab anyone the way she has about Allison Ritz this week. Usually Sabrina is popular, but tame and leaves most kids alone, but the way she has been talking to her friends about the Liberty Grammar girls has gotten Shannon and I a bit curious as to what is going on.

I do not know. Shannon, Robert, David, and I all find the whole thing quite funny, and Robert even commented that he cannot believe that Sabrina's never had a run in with the Liberty Grammar kids before. Are you kidding me? Shannon and I are thinking that too.

I sure have had many issues with the Liberty Grammar girls! Trust me, so has Shannon. Robert, and David, also cannot stand anyone from Liberty Grammar. It is a bit different for me as those girls hate me because Leanne hates me, and we know each other from being forced to play together due to our mums and at work functions and I cannot stand Leanne Cummingo! She also cannot stand me and by association Leanne's friends hate me too, especially Allison Ritz. Leanne also hates Shannon due to their association with me and Robert and David too. All we ever do is argue with them.

I do not know. Sabrina is usually harmless and so her friends, although she has always been extremely popular at school. We are friends with Sabrina, although not overly close.

Enough on that though! My friends stayed over to around 10:00pm and their parents picked them up. We had a good night and enjoyed each other's company. I went to bed around 11:00pm and said goodnight to my parents and then went to bed.

…

On Saturday, my dad drove me to the basketball stadium. Since mum is working. Mum works a lot of weekends and is a wedding photographer. I do not mind spending time with dad, and he enjoys coming to watch me play basketball and is proud of what I have achieved in sport over the years.

I have been playing basketball for 3 years and play socially for a basketball club and at school for the grade 5/6 team. I spend a lot of time training and playing basketball and it takes up more time and energy for me than swimming does. I just swim for the school team and enjoy it, but basketball is my main passion.

My dad drove me up to the local basketball stadium and I went and said hi to the coach and went to the locker rooms to get changed and said hi to my friend Anna, who is also on the team, and a few other friends.
I really like Anna! She is great and is one of my closest friends and Anna is good friends with Shannon, Robert, and David too. Anna does not go to school with us but and goes to Rydall primary school and is one of the few friends of ours from that school. Since Robert, Shannon, David, and I all play sport a few of our friends are from Rydal primary school.

Rydall primary school is the closest public primary school to Jefferson primary school and is near to us. It only takes about 20-30 minutes by bus or car to get to. Which is close for a rural area. It is still further out than my school though and my parents have always sent me to Jefferson primary school. Rydall primary school is in the nearest town to us, and Ivory Grammar is there too. Both adults and kids go between the towns all the time for school, work or fun and that town boasts a much larger shopping center then ours, so that is the main reason to go there socially. Or to visit friends.

The two towns are fierce rivals though for everything and are extremely competitive. Especially when it comes to sport, school and work and sales for adults and both towns boast that they are more popular with tourists too. Jefferson primary school and Rydall primary school compete with everything of course. The two schools do not get along for the most part, although the relationship between our school's is nowhere near as bad as with Liberty Grammar.

I have friends from Rydall primary school and so do Robert, Shannon and David. One of our best friends goes there actually. Although not a lot of other kids at our school have friends from there. A lot of the Rydall Secondary kids do not like kids from our school. Since there is rivalry between our schools. The popular kids from the school's do not mix, particularly Sabrina and Matts group, do not play with anyone from the other town. As my friends and I are friends with Anna we are friendly with her whole group from Rydall Secondary and on good terms with them. They are remarkably similar to us. Anna's friends Michelle, Tanya, Tom, and Alex are nice and are all friends of ours. Tom and Alex play social soccer with Robert outside school and Michelle is on the basketball team with Anna and me.

Anna and I are good friends and she get along great with Shannon too and Robert and David. I am the closest to Anna in the group though and we have a lot in common. Anna and I have basketball in common and Anna is one of the best female players at Rydall primary school and is my main competition from that school in the school comp! We play on rival school teams and Anna's a hot shot player and team captain at her school. Anna and I are competitive, but also friends and we play on the after-school team together on the same team, as that is mixed between both towns, and we travel all over for competitions. It is not easy to get onto that basketball team and is considered a privilege. We often travel to other towns to play.

Anna is friends with my whole group and the closest female friend that Shannon and I have. A lot closer than Sabrina Brewer's group. Anna is always coming over to my place or Shannon's at the weekends and is good friends with Robert and David too. Anna is as into sports and video games as I am or Shannon and is very sporty. She also has many male friends too at school. We have been friends for a few years now and Anna is one of the gang with my group and I wish she went to school with us, but Jefferson primary school is not close to Anna.

Anna said hi to me and we got changed. I put on my blue basketball uniform and headed out and the coach got us to warm up and pass balls to each other and we were practicing free throws too. I could see the other team warming up too.

Once the game started, I took my place near the goals, since I am tall. We are playing an out-of-town team and my social team is mixed between my town and the next town over and the team we are playing is mixed between two other towns that are about an hour away and they brought their team over by bus. It is a large competition involving lots of teams.

We played a mean game, and I was happy when I got a three pointer in the first 10 minutes and then the other team scored a couple more. I am competitive with basketball and like to win. My friend Anna is also doing well and scored a three pointer too.

By half time, the scores were 30/25 in our favor, which is a bit too close for comfort, but we are an evenly matched team. Our coach sat us on the bench and drilled us on the game so far and told us what we needed to do. I took a drink from my water bottle. I was stuffed! I am having fun though.

I was on again for the second half and usually do not get much bench time since I am a talented player. We ran onto the courts and were all determined to win. If we win this game, then we will be in the semi- final.

The second half was good, although my opponent was rough and as she was going for the ball, it knocked me over. I was fine, although I fell and was not injured or anything, but I was pissed! That was not on, and I was glad when she got fouled. I got two free throws for that and sank one of the baskets, which I was happy with and then we were on a winning streak after that. I scored another basket and so did a couple of other girls.

We ended up winning the game 50/35. Which was fantastic and meant that we are now in the semifinal. The coach congratulated everyone and said we did an excellent job and reminded everyone to be at training. I went out with my dad and just drove back home and said hi to friends after I finished training. No-one is going out today, although occasionally we will have pizza after a big win. I headed home, still ecstatic about my win!

Chapter 9

Robert

At school on Tuesday, we had school assembly, which we do once a week and this was going to be an important assembly because the school captains are getting voted in. Since the school year just started and we are getting a male and female school captain.

I do not really care either way and I am not going for school captain or wanted to be in the running. I have a lot on my plate as it is at school and after school, but I am happy.

Anyway! So hi, my name is Robert Mariano and I just turned 12 years old, and I go to Jefferson primary school and am in grade six. I do not mind school and have some great friends there. Namely Stacey, Shannon, and David. We are close and spend a lot of time together. At school we are inseparable and after school we often go to each other's houses and play together at the weekends and our parents are all friends too.

I have no issues with being friends with girls and Stacey Green and Shannon Chambers are my two best friends. We go way back! Trust me and I have known Stacey and Shannon since we were babies and we have been inseparable all our lives and grew up together.
David is my only male friend really and we are close. It was great when David moved to town two years ago! When we were in grade four and 9 years old. David is great and we are inseparable, and David is also close to Stacey and Shannon and like me has no issues with having his closest friends being girls.

David and I cop a lot of teasing about that though! From boys at school, although this year they do not tease us as much. Since the popular boys are also starting to play with the girls at lunch, they cannot really tease us about playing with Stacey and Shannon. Until last year we used to get teased about it though and asked why we do not play with the boys at lunch. I did not care though and neither did David.
It is really those idiots Peter and Sam that are the worst at teasing us! Seriously, I hate those two and so does David. They are always picking on Stacey and Shannon, which I do not appreciate, and I am protective of Stacey and Shannon, they are like sisters to me and to David too. Peter and Sam were always teasing us when we were younger and used to tease me too and David, but they would be brave to do that this year! They know that. I am like a head taller than Peter or Sam now and so is David and I also know how to fight, so they had better not mess

with us! Or Stacey or Shannon either.

I do not know! I Enjoy spending time with my friends and as a group we are all sporty. I play soccer and ride my bike a lot. We all enjoy video games and Stacey, and Shannon are tomboys and keep up with David and me.

I live with my parents and little brother Sal. Who is only 3 years old, and he is super cute! Although very cheeky, I adore my little brother and am glad I have finally got a sibling after all these years. I am 8 years older than Sal. I come from a big extended family and have a cousin Daniel who is the same age as me, but lives in Melbourne. We are still close though and talk all the time on the internet and phone and visit each other when we can. All my cousins, aunts, uncles, and grandparents live in Melbourne. My mum, dad, brother, and I are the only ones in Queensland, but we visit Melbourne at least twice a year.

...

Enough on that though! At school on Tuesday the teacher rounded up our class to go to assembly. We do that first thing on Tuesday morning, and everyone hates those assemblies! They are so boring, but we do it every week.

We lined up in two lines and waited for the principal to come out and sat in chairs in the school gym. As we are in grade six, we sit up at the back and the younger kids are towards the front. The teachers sit on the edge of their class sections.

The principal made some announcements and talked about some school events that are coming up and then it was finally time to announce the new school captains. Which is important and the school captains are from grade six, although each grade gets a class captain. There is always a male and female school captain to be fair.

The principal made the announcement and said that this year's girls school captain is Sabrina Brewer, and the boys captain is Matt Smithers. Sabrina got voted in! Also Matt. Sabrina has been wanting this all-last year and was grade five class captain last year and she has always been popular, so it was not surprising that she got voted. Sabrina's all right. We are casual friends and live on the same street, so we occasionally play together. Matt is extremely popular too and a sports star at school, but we do not get along. He is another one of the popular boys that hangs out with Peter and Sam. My group does not like him!

So, after the school captain announcements, the principal broke up the assembly and the teacher brought us back to class and we are working on math's and English this morning. Which is getting harder, since we are in grade six and then at recess and lunch, I played sport and spent time with my friends. Sabrina and Matt were near to us and were talking excitedly about getting voted school captains. The popular boys and girls play together quite a bit this year, but not all the time.

After lunch and then sports class that afternoon my mum picked me up, since she is not working today, and my dad is taking care of the shop. (My parents own a pet shop). My mum and dad rotate that and if the shop is busy then they both work and I go to after school care and Sal is in childcare, but mum prefers to stay with Sal and I and only works part time now. Two days a week until Sal goes to school. I said hi to mum and Sal was in the front seat and I said hi and Sal was excited to see me, like he always is.

We drove home and I played with Sal a bit. He is a typical little boy that enjoys toys, and we were playing with a new toy truck that Sal loves, and I like it too and do not mind spending time with my little brother after school and we were having fun playing and Sal is telling me all his stories. We then watched some cartoons and mum was preparing dinner and I helped by setting the table and mum asked me how school was. I adore my mum and we are close, and I am close to my dad too.

Dad came home and we had dinner and I worked on some homework. It was a good night, and we always watched the news and a couple of television shows and Sal goes to bed earlier than me at 7:30pm, but I stay up until 10:00pm on school nights. I crashed into bed and was not looking forward to school tomorrow, but what can you do?

Chapter 10

Stacey

I was annoyed on Saturday afternoon when my mum announced that we were going to visit Leanne's house. Are you serious? Did I have to go with her? Of course, I did. Since I am only 12 years old, and mum does not want me at home by myself all day and dad are off playing golf with some work friends. I did not even have basketball or swimming as an excuse. Since I have no basketball games this weekend and my swim meet is next weekend. I also have a basketball game next week, so I am busy next week and had been looking forward to a weekend off this week and now mum wants me to go Leanne and Marie's house to visit. Although mum said Marie will not be there. Just Leanne's mum and Leanne.

This is simply great seriously! I am really getting sick of mum forcing me to visit Leanne and her parents and my dad too. If we are going to go to visit someone, why can't we go to Shannon or Robert's houses? My mum is super close to their parents and that gives me a chance to spend time with Robert or Shannon, but no! Not today.

My mum is close to Leanne's mum and dad and so is my dad. They are good friends. Unlike us daughters! Mum often goes to visit Leanne's mum and makes me come with her.
My mum is close to Leanne's mum and dad and so is my dad. They are good friends. Unlike us daughters! Mum often goes to visit Leanne's mum and makes me come with her.

I really hate going to Leanne's house! Seriously. I have known Leanne Cummingo for years, since our dads started working together when we were about 7 years old. We have never gotten along though. Not since we were little. When we are forced to go to each other's houses we never play together or talk. Leanne is usually either watching television and ignoring me or playing with her toys, but she will not let me near her stuff! Trust me and we usually get into an argument when I come over. Since that w… is always teasing me.

So, my mum drove me over to Leanne's place on Gresham Avenue. Or snob central as my friends and I call it.

Gresham Avenue is on the wealthy side of town and is where the rich families live and is full of mansions and Leanne's family lives in a mansion on Gresham Avenue. I have been there with my mum before. My mum drove me to Leanne's, and we chatted lively along the way. I love my mum; we get along great.

I do not hold it against my parents that I am forced to go to Leanne's house and hate it. I know my mum is close to Leanne's mum and I like Leanne's parents myself and they are always nice to me, but it is their daughters that are the problem! Leanne and Marie are both idiots.

My mum pulled up in front of Leanne's parents place and it is a huge mansion that is twice the size of my house and I know that Leanne's parents have full time help at the house and Leanne is looked after by a housekeeper/babysitter and there is also a gardener and a chauffeur too. Stupid snobs! I know that Leanne and her sister are completely spoilt by their mum and dad and love money.

Mum went up to the door and rang the doorbell and Leanne's mum answered and said hi to my mum and I and said that I am getting very pretty and asked how I am too.

I walked into the house with my mum. My mum is chatting lively with Leanne's mum, and we walked in and went into the kitchen, where there are some snacks and drinks, and Leanne was in the kitchen having something to eat when I came in with mum. Leanne said hi to my mum and to me and was only being nice to me because her mum and my mum were there, although I know that she hates me and my friends. I said hi back and had something to eat. There were some sandwiches and a snack of chips, and I know that it would have been prepared by the housekeeper, who was hovering around the kitchen and helping.

Like most of the families on Gresham Avenue Leanne's family has full-time help and Leanne's mum is a hot-shoot lawyer and has worked full-time since Leanne was one year old. Her dad is a lawyer too and her parents run their own firm, but they also come from family money and do not have to work, but they want to work and enjoy being solicitors.

Leanne's mum does no housework or cooking, neither does her dad and I know it, or gardening and Leanne and her sister were looked after by a babysitter since they were babies. Leanne has never had to do any chores or housework and will never have to. Leanne's family are wealthy and proud of their money and are not embarrassed about having help in the house. In fact, they brag about it. They even have a family chauffeur. The chauffeur is for Leanne and her sister as Leanne's parents can drive and both own expensive cars, but Leanne and Marie do not drive.

I honestly cannot begin to understand living in a house like Leanne's! Or Allison Ritz's either. Who has a mansion even larger than Leanne's, with as much help around the house. I come from quite a normal middle-class family and my parents provide well for me, but we certainly are not rice enough to live on Gresham Avenue or to hire help around the house and my mum stayed home with me till kindergarten and then sent me to after school care.

This is where the problem between me and Leanne arises of course and not just Leanne and I but anyone from my school and Allison and Leanne and their friends at Liberty Grammar. It is not just that Leanne and Allison are rich. They are also the biggest snobs I have ever met. Leanne will not even talk to anyone that does not live on Gresham Avenue or a beachside mansion, goes to her school and absolutely cannot stand public school kids and neither can Allison. I am the same as them though. I cannot stand Liberty Grammar snobs, especially Leanne and Allison and am proud to be a middle school public schooler and my mum needs to understand that Leanne and I are never going to get along and so does my dad, but they keep bringing me to her house and trying to get us to play together. It annoys both Leanne and me.

We visited for a while and Leanne, and I left our mums to it in the kitchen having a good chat and they told us to go out to the backyard if we wanted to play.

Great! The last thing I want to do is go spend time with Leanne on my own, although we are being forced into it by our mums who tell us to go outside when they want to spend time on their own, but I do not mind that. Leanne's house is great, and they have a dog outside too, which is fun, and Leanne and I usually just stick to doing our own things and do not play together when I come over and really cannot stand being forced to go over to each other's houses.

I went outside with Leanne, and we did not really talk but walked out together and Leanne got the dog. Since we both enjoy playing with him, about the only thing we have in common! Leanne's dog is a cute toy dog that is a little Pomeranian, and it is small and very friendly and enjoys getting patted. The dog's name is Max, and he is super spoilt.

I played with the dog for ages. Patting him and getting him to do tricks and Leanne and I were both playing with him, but Max I think was getting tired with the game and had something to eat. Leanne and I thought that we gave him enough exercise! Although it was fun playing with him and I like animals, especially dogs.

So, what to do now? Without Max as a distraction Leanne and I only had each other to spend time with, which is always awkward. I really cannot stand that snob! Seriously, and my mum is always forcing me to play with Leanne.
I tried to be friendly though and asked Leanne if she had a soccer or basketball game we could play with, or if we could ask our mums to go for a walk down in the park. Which I know is not far.

I was trying! It is so awkward anytime I go to Leanne's house and my mum I always at me to try to be friendlier with Leanne.

Leanne Cummingo was no help though! Seriously and just gave a laugh and spoke.

"Really! You want to go to the park with me? No way is that going to happen. One of my friends might see us."

That was rude and I only suggested the park to get us out of the house and to give us something to do. Clearly Leanne does not want her snobby Liberty Grammar friends to see her spending time with me and I am not surprised. I would not want my friends to see me playing with Leanne Cummingo either. They all hate her.
I am not scared of Leanne and am annoyed at that comment. She is always saying something like that to me! When I come past Leanne's always teasing me and calling me names. I did not back down and asked Leanne.

"What's that supposed to mean?"

Leanne rolled her eyes and spoke.

"You heard me! You think I want Allison or my other friends seeing me with a public-school girl that does not wear decent clothes."

Who does Leanne think is talking to me like that? Stupid snob. I have been nothing but nice to her or trying to today, but that snob does not care, and I know that she hates me and my friends.

I was annoyed at the comment and exclaimed back to Leanne.

"Well, I would not like my friends to see me with you either. Why would I want to play with some private school snob that has the biggest idiots for friends I have ever seen! Especially Allison."

I knew that would piss Leanne off! She is very close to Allison and hates being called a snob, although the only reason I called her that is because she is insulting me.

Leanne and I of course got into an argument after that! A bad one. We're always arguing and it does not take much to start one. I was holding my own and screaming at Leanne and calling her names and she was just as bad.

Finally after about 10 minutes of arguing Leanne hit me! Oh my God! What the hell? Even though I've been in many arguments with Leanne, we have never gotten physical about it. Leanne had pushed me back and slapped me. Which made me laugh actually! Who slaps? That is way too girly for me. I am a tomboy and Leanne is not very smart starting me. I know how to fight and if she wants a fight then she will get it! No problem.

As soon as Leanne slapped me I retaliated straight away and I think that I surprised her when I gave her a hard push back and she stumbled and fell. Well she started it! We were on grass and I don't think that that would hurt too much. We rolled about and Leanne is clearly a goer for fights and has no issues getting into them.

Considering that it is my first official fight I thought that I was doing pretty well. I pushed Leanne back and gave her a hit too, although I gave her a slap and not a punch, like I would in a normal fight. I am not that bad that I would punch someone which if they have not punched me. Since a punch would be a harder hit.

We rolled about and all those wrestling lessons from Robert and Shannon are paying off. Leanne is up for a fight and I think that she might be regretting hitting me, although the fight is on now and I copped another slap from Leanne. Which hurt.

Alright that is it! Leanne got up off me and looked pleased with herself. Although I knew that the fight is not over and that she is just waiting for me to get up. We have had enough of rolling around on the grass. Once I was up grabbed I Leanne and turned her around. I am stronger than her and that was not hard! Since Leanne is skinny. I turned her around and had her in a grip and kicked Leanne on the leg. Time to stop with those stupid slaps! I want a real fight and Robert and David would laugh if they thought of the cat fight that this started off as. I knew that that kick hurt and was glad and Leanne called me a complete b…! For kicking her.

Well she started it! This is after years of Leanne and her older sister Marie teasing me and Leanne hitting me today is the last straw. Leanne recovered quickly from that kick. It was not that hard anyway, but it really pissed Leanne off! She came and pushed me back again and kicked me on the shin too. Ow! That is going to bruise.

After that kicked I jumped Leanne and pushed her back on the grass and we were rolling about and I got Leanne again with another hit, this time on the arm. Both of us are going to have some bruises tomorrow! We were still in the middle of a fight and causing a commotion when the doors to the backyard opened and my mum and Leanne's mum came running out and mum was just in time to see Leanne roll me over and get her hand up to punch me I think! At least that is what it looks like.

That stupid b…! Seriously. Leanne did not get a chance to punch me but because we both heard our mum's come outside and my mum was furious! So was Leanne's mum and my mum exclaimed.

"What's going on girls? You need to stop fighting now!"

We did stop fighting. Leanne's not that brave that she would punch me in front of her mum, although this whole fight should not have happened and I know that I am going to be in big trouble with my parents and so is Leanne. Not that I care about that! Well Leanne started it! Seriously. I would not have hit her or retaliated if she hadn't of hit me in the first place.

Leanne got up off me and did not need to be pulled off and I also got up. My mum came over and asked if I am okay, but yelled at me and exclaimed that she cannot believe what happened and was very angry at Leanne too and was also yelling at her and Leanne's mum joined in and asked what happened and why we are fighting.

I was pissed at Leanne and did not want to talk to her! Our mum's separated us straight away and mum took me for a talk and asked me what happened and I said that Leanne hit me after we got into an argument and I was just defending myself. I do not know what Leanne was telling her mum, but my mum was quick to get annoyed at that one and went storming up to Leanne and her mum with me following. My mum asked Leanne if she hit me first and Leanne said yes, because I was calling her names and I said that Leanne was calling me names too.

Leanne's mum exclaimed.

"Leanne! How could you hit Stacey? You need to apologise."

Leanne gave me a look and exclaimed.

"I am not apologising to her! She hit me back and called me names."

"I do not want to apologise to you either."

I exclaimed back to Leanne

This of course led to another argument and our mums were not having much luck with Leanne and I! Although I was just pissed and Leanne and I are as bad as each other in an argument. Mum just said to Leanne's mum.

"We need to separate them. I will take Stacey home." Leanne's mum said.

"I think that that is for the best. I am sorry this happened. Leanne is going to be in big trouble."

"So is Stacey."

My mum said and that she would be in contact with Leanne's mum.

My mum and I did leave the house and Leanne did not say bye to me Which was definitely not a surprise after the fight, although Leanne's mum did say bye. We left and I felt bad about ruining my mum's visit with Leanne's mum, although Leanne started it! I was angry at her.

Mum took me out to the car and told me to get in. I could tell that she is not happy with me and once we were in the car she exclaimed to me.

"Stacey, this behaviour is not good enough. I cannot believe that you got into a fight with Leanne."

I said to mum that I know, but Leanne hit me and I was just reacting. Mum asked what happened and if I am ok. I can tell that she is worried about me. I am fine, just worse for wear. The slaps definitely hurt and so did the kick. I was not happy and I know that Leanne got hurt too and she deserves it! For hitting me in the first place. I would not have reacted if she had not of hit me.

Mum drove me home and said that I am not allowed to have any friends over for the rest of the week and am under punishment, including doing chores around the house and she said that she never wants to see me get into another fight like that again.

Awesome! Thanks Leanne. I went into the lounge and mum got me some ice for my lip and also told me to relax. I was very shaken up and annoyed and just want to relax tonight. I thought that this is the finish of the trouble with Leanne and the Liberty Grammar girls. How could I not know that the trouble had just begun!

Part 2-Troube begins between the schools

Shannon

Chapter 11

At school on Monday morning I was talking to my best friend Stacey Green about what happened with her and Leanne Cummingo over the weekend. Robert and David were listening in too. The teacher had not arrived yet and on Monday everyone likes to talk about the weekend and my friends and I sure do. We were sitting outside with the rest of the kids from before care.

I go to before and after school care five days a week, since my parents work full time and so do Robert, Shannon and David. Sabrina Brewer is also in before and after school care. So before school I was sitting next to the playground with Stacey, Robert and David and we were talking. Like all the grade six kids are. We were watching the little kids playing on the playground.

I do not mind playing on the playground, but this one is designed for the little kids. It is for grade preps to 2's and the one next to it is grade 3's and 4's. So the big kids are not allowed on this playground. We do not mind just watching the little ones play and talking to each other though in the morning. My friends and I are nearly in high school anyway. There were child care workers watching us in the morning until the teachers come out. I am looking forward to next year when I am in high school and do not need to go to after school care, but my parents still do not prefer me to be home on my own yet after school.

So I was sitting with my friends and Stacey was talking to us about what happen with Leanne Cumming on the weekend and the fight they had. Stacey was sitting next to me and talking loudly about how angry she is with Leanne. Stacey was quite animated Monday morning and annoyed and said that she actually got hit by Leanne on Saturday and they got into a fight and Stacey's mum and Leanne's stopped the fight before it got too far. Although Stacey said that Leanne was about to punch her when their mum's broke up the fight.

I know all this anyway because Stacey rang Robert, David and I on the weekend and said that she is not able to catch up on the weekend, although on Sunday we had been planning to go to the beach. Stacey said that she was grounded all weekend. So she has not seen any of us since Friday and was explaining the story this morning as we hung out and talked, although I knew she got into a fight with Leanne and is in trouble with her parents.

Oh honestly! I was angry listening to Stacey and do not blame Stacey for hitting Leanne back and getting into a fight with her. That Leanne is such a stuck up snob! Like all of the Liberty Grammar kids are. Stacey was talking about it and we all agreed Leanne is an idiot and deserved to be hit back.

Sabrina Brewer was sitting with the rest of the popular girls in a group not far from us and the popular boys are playing a game of soccer. Sabrina could hear Stacey and I though.

...

Stacey and I were having a good chat and were talking to each other when Sabrina came over. She could hear us from where she was sitting and got interested in our conversation and so did her friends.

 Robert and David were talking to each other and didn't mind when Sabrina invited Stacey and I over to where she was sitting with the other popular girls from the class. Since she wants the gossip and usually Sabrina's group is girls only, although they sometimes play with the boys, but not all the time and this morning the popular boys are busy playing soccer on the other side of the playground and Robert and David were not with them. They do not get along with those guys. Especially Peter, Sam and Matt.

Sabrina Brewer is very popular at school and just got voted school captain. Max is the boy's school captain. Sabrina was popular before she got voted school captain, but now everyone knows her at school and apparently she won by a landslide. I don't mind talking to Sabrina's friends. They are nice to me and my friends. Elise is particularly nice out of the group.

So Stacey and I went and sat with Sabrina and her friends and told Robert and David we would be back. They were busy talking anyway and did not mind.

Sabrina said hi and asked Stacey what happened with Leanne. We all know that Sabrina hates the liberty Grammar girls. All the girls in our class do, especially Sabrina's group after Sabrina's famous argument with Allison at The Avenue. We all know that Leanne is Allison Ritz's best friend and they are really close, but both of them are stuck up snobs.

Sabrina said to Stacey well done and asked her about the fight. Stacey was talking about it and Sabrina was impressed and said that Leanne deserved it and the other girls laughed at that one. We were having fun, but the bell rang and the child care workers were gathering everyone up and we went into class. Ready to start the school day.

....

My name is Shannon Chambers by the way and I just turned 12 years old and I am in grade six at Jefferson primary school. I am an only child and am very close to my parents and have no brothers, sisters or cousins. So I am the only kid of my family. I do have grandparent's on both sides, although my mum is adopted and they are my adoptive grandparent's, but that does not matter.

My best friends are Stacey Green and Robert Mariano and David is another very close friend, although we have only known each other since grade four. David got close to Stacey, Robert and I quickly though and we are all inseparable at school and outside school.

I really love Stacey and Robert! We have definitely grown up together and I have known Stacey since we were babies and we are still very close and I think that we always will be. Stacey is like a sister to me and we always say that we are close enough to be sisters. Stacey is a tomboy like me and we enjoy sports, wrestling, riding around on bikes and rollerblades and spend most of our time with Robert and David, instead of the girls in our class. Although we are friends with Sabrina Brewer and her friends.

Robert is also great and I have known Robert as long as I have known Stacey Green. Robert is like the brother I never had and we are very close. Robert is very protective of Stacey and I and has never minded that we are girls. We have been best friends since we were running around in nappies and are all still very close. I grew up going to

Stacey and Robert's houses and am close with both Stacey and Robert's parents and also think that Robert's little brother Sal is very cute.

David came into the picture in grade 4 and he was new to town and became friends with Robert, Stacey and I quickly. We spend heaps of time together at school and also on weekends. So that is my group! I am happy with my friends and my life in my little town.

As I started working on some work the teacher was handing out. I was looking forward to going home. It is going to be a long day at school.

Chapter 12

Stacey

On Sunday Morning my mum and dad drove me over to the swimming pool for my big swim meet. This is the main swim meet for the school swimming squad. Involving grade five to year 8 kids and there are older kids competing in other races too.

I really enjoy swimming carnivals and compete in them whenever the school has them. Which is around 3 times a year. I am doing the freestyle race and the relay. Which is always and freestyle is my best stroke. The whole team stays the whole day so we can support our teammates. The girl's events are all this morning and the boys are just after us for grade six to year 8 kids and the older high school kids are going this afternoon.

I was not in the first couple of races, but sat in the stands next to my teammates to watch other kids compete. They did the backstroke first and then breaststroke for the girls. There is one race for each stroke, since there are quite a few kids racing today. The girl that won the backstroke won by a lot and the backstroke was a closer leg.

It was finally my turn and my coach gathered up us girls that were racing in the freestyle. I am quite used to racing by now, although I can be competitive. I got behind the start mark, after taking off my tracksuit and put my goggles on. Then got behind the starting platform like the other girls were. The referee yelled. Ready, get set go and I dived into the pool like my coach taught me. I am getting quite good at that now, although that technique took a while to learn and coach works hard on that with us.

The race is just one lap and we are expected to go fast and I took off with a hit and was doing a steady freestyle and was determined. I knew that there are a few really strong swimmers in this race. I swan well and Alexa right on my side for most of the race, but I took it out pretty easily and towards the end I pushed in front and won by a half a head! Alexa is a good swimmer and gave me a good race. I still won though and I was thrilled! Yay. I did not know the other swimmer. I think she is from Rydal primary school and looks to be the same age as me, but there are two from my school too.

I got up out of the pool and the coach said great job and so did my parents. Who came down the bleachers to say good job. I went up to collect my ribbon and so did the other two winners and they were handing them out, not doing a presentation or anything, but they said congratulations to be. I have one more race to go and did not get a lot of time to relax! Although there is one more race before I do the relay.

The first relay is the mixed relay with one swimmer for each stroke. I am not in that one. We are only allowed to race in one relay swim I decided on the freestyle one and will be the last to swim.

The first relay was fun to watch, although Rydal primary and Secondary school took out the race, although it was close. The last morning girls race was the freestyle relay and I was in that race. It is one lap for each girl and I am going last. The race started and our racer was doing well, she pulled in front a bit, but Rydal primary school was close to us. By the end of the lap she had just pulled up right in front. The second swimmer fell behind a bit and the race was pretty much neck and neck for most of the race with the swimmer from Rydal Secondary College. The third swimmer to race was good from our team and it was Alexa. she pretty much goes first and second with me for most races. When she jumped in the water Alexa was just in front of the other girl.

They had a great race and we pulled in front of the other team. The rest of the team were urging her on. We want to win! Especially after the last relay's result. I was last to swim and dived straight in and was head to head with the last girl from Rydal Secondary College. This girl is in Year 7 I think and I have raced her before. It was a good race between us two! It was pretty much neck and neck right to the end, but I got her in the end. By like half a head! I was super exited and my parents and friends were going crazy and so was my coach. We collected our ribbons. It was a great race for us!

After the race I headed back to the change rooms to get changed. It had been an exciting day and I was not staying to watch the boys or older high school kids race. It is a long day otherwise and I want to go over to Shannon's house this afternoon. Mum said that that is fine and Robert and David are coming too.

I got changed into some jeans and a t-shirt after a shower and packed my swim bag. I said bye to my friends and the coach and my parents drove me home. I was still ecstatic about my wins today!

Chapter 13

Allison

On Monday at school my best friend Leanne was telling me all about what happened with Stacey Green from Jefferson primary school last weekend and my friends and I were angry and let Leanne backstab Stacey and let it out and Leanne exclaimed that that blond b… Leanne actually hit Stacey and they got into a fight after an argument, although Leanne admitted that she was first to hit and Stacey just reacted to that and is clearly a bit of a goer when it comes to fights.

I was proud of Leanne and am not angry at her at hitting Stacey. Actually I think that Stacey Green deserves it like the rest of the Jefferson primary school girls do.

I do not know what it is with those idiots that go to Jefferson primary school, but this is not the only trouble with them recently and my group at school is getting really sick of it.

My name is Allison Ritz and I am 12 years old and am in grade six at Liberty Grammar. I live with my parents and twin brother Aaron. Aaron is my twin brother and we are twins. Aaron goes to the same school as me. Since it is co-ed. My parents and I are close and they definitely spoil my brother and I. I come from a very wealthy family and I my parents are Japanese and so am I. My parents come from family money, but also work hard and run a successful range of shops.

I like being a rich kid and live in a large mansion on Gresham Avenue, with my parents and brother and we have a live in housekeeper, a nanny, gardener and my parents also have a chauffeur. The nanny will not be there once Aaron and I start high school though and I know that I will miss her. She has been looking after us since we were babies and my mum has always worked full time and appreciates the help.

I go to private school and Liberty Grammar is an expensive school that mostly the wealthy families in town send their kids too, unless they are scholarship students

I have a good group at school and mainly hang out with girls, although because I have a twin brother I know all of Aaron's friends too. Although I don't play with them much at school. There is definitely the girls group and the guys group in the popular group at school.

Aaron plays mostly with boys at school and not usually with my group at lunch and recess and particularly when we were younger Aaron would not let me play with his group at school, although we are close and spend a lot of time together at home. This year the girls mainly stick together at lunch and recess still and do not join the boys with playing sport at recess, although we occasionally watch them play sport. We like to gossip at lunch and play on the playground, although not so much this year. I am starting to feel like a teenager now and am looking forward to moving into the high school at Liberty Grammar. One more year to go!

I am very popular at school and have been friends with the same group of girls since grade prep and Leanne Cummingo is my best friend. Leanne is great and we have been friends our whole lives. Since Leanne grew up across the road from me. Leanne is friends with me and also thinks that my brother Aaron is a nice guy and we all used to play together on the street as little kids and Leanne grew up coming over to my house and me to hers.

Leanne's sister is nice too and I like Marie. She is great and is cool, since she is older than us and a teenager. Leanne is very popular at school and is unofficially second in charge to me with our group. The girls in the popular group already listen to Leanne and I and we decide who is in and out and in the primary school part of Liberty Grammar and our group are all the most popular girls in our grade six class. I have my close friends and Ally, Laticia and Monica in the group too. We have all been friends since grade prep and there is a big group of us at school.

My brother Aaron is also very popular and his best friend is Mitch, who I also know really well and Mitch grew up coming over to our house like Leanne did.

The group at Liberty Grammar are all the popular kids at school and we all come from wealthy families. I do not hang out with public school kids and certainly cannot stand anyone from Jefferson primary school and lately there has been more trouble with those girls then previously.

Mainly because of that Sabrina Brewer! Also Stacey Green from Jefferson Secondary College. I have just met Sabrina Brewer recently and so has Leanne, but wow! I hated Sabrina on sight when I met her over at The Avenue. I went over to The Avenue with Leanne and her older sister Marie and my older cousin Lara for the teen party. Which I am not allowed to go to unless I am there with older kids and neither is Leanne. Since my parents want me to be safe.

Sabrina was there with her older sisters Monica and Sandra. I have heard about Monica from Marie and so has Leanne. Monica is a piece of work and hates all the Liberty Grammar girls and there is a lot of trouble in the year 10 class between Liberty Grammar and Jefferson Secondary College. When we were at The Avenue my cousin Lara and Marie got into an argument with Monica and then I got into one with Sabrina and I was just teasing her for fun and so was Leanne. We did not mean for things to go as far as it did. The argument was pretty bad!

Sabrina Brewer sure surprised me! Also Leanne. We have discussed this afterwards. Sabrina looks pretty harmless with her blond hair, blue eyes and dimples and she is skinny and very pretty, although I would never tell her that after our argument.

After I insulted Sabrina and her friends Grace and Sophie she lashed out at me straight away. I only teased them because of Marie and my cousins argument with Monica and her friend and I was angry about that and Sabrina was angry too. Grace and Sophie stayed quite, but Sabrina and I got into a huge public argument. Clearly Sabrina is no wallflower in an argument and can match it with me and she also is not scared of me either and trust me Sabrina would be brave to hit me! I know how to fight, since I grew up with a twin brother. Aaron taught me lots of tricks and we used to play fight all the time until this year.

I did a big of digging about Sabrina after that and learnt a lot about her! Sounds like Sabrina Brewer is school captain at Jefferson primary school and is very popular. She mainly hangs out with girls, but there are guys in the group too.

Sounds like my group has some competition and Leanne and I have talked at length regarding the Jefferson primary school girls, particularly Stacey Green and Sabrina Brewer. Stacey is another piece of work and she had some nerve getting into a fight with Leanne and Stacey has always been trouble with Leanne and I since we were kids and things just escalated this year and Shannon Chambers is just as bad.

Leanne and I agree that we will not start anything with those girls unless they start us and I have not seen Sabrina Brewer since our argument at The Avenue, although I hate her already.

...

Enough on that though! After school my nanny picked me and up went home with Aaron and I. I do not play any after school sport, although I get piano lessons, since my parents wanted me to be in an activity. I do not mind playing piano. I prefer it to playing sports, or dancing, which I have never been into.

My nanny dropped Aaron and I off and was still at the house cleaning and helping the housekeeper. We have two live at home workers at the moment for the house. The nanny and housekeeper and also a full time gardener/Handyman. The nanny is only here until the end of the year though and then she will be dismissed once Aaron and I start high school. Since we do not need two housekeepers. I will miss my nanny, although I am getting old for that now and even this year I do not need much watching and neither does my brother.

I went straight up to my room to get changed into some tracksuit pants and relax in front of the television. I have my own television and computer in my room.

I turned on the television and watched on of my favourite cartoons. Which is fun after school. I did not think about school anymore. I just want to relax a bit.

Chapter 14

Sabrina

On Saturday afternoon I had finished dance class and was playing with my friends at the playground near the beach with my friends Grace, Sophie, Elise, Emma, Charlotte and Amy.

Dance class was great and is starting to get harder. I am still in junior squad, since I am 12 years old, but I will be moving up to seniors next year and I am looking forward to it. I love dancing and have been dancing since I was a little girl and still love it. I do ballet, contemporary, lyrical, tap jazz and hip hop and also do acrobatics. Which is my favourite style.

I dance 6 hours a week and two hours Saturday morning and Monday, Tuesday, Wednesday and Friday 1 hour each day. It's a lot of training, but we're a competitive dance school. A few of my school friends are also in my dance class, but Elise plays basketball.

…

I was having fun with my friends and we were sitting on the equipment and talking. My mum was there with Grace and Sophie's mum at The Avenue, but they were at the nearby café place and could see us from there, but they were not keeping a big watch on us. Mum still does not like me heading out on my own too much and takes me to all my dance classes and competitions anyway and says that she enjoys being a dance mum. Mum used to dance at my age too.

I was glad for this freedom at least and being able to talk to my friends. We are nearly teenagers anyway and I know that next year I will have more freedom when I start high school, like my sisters do.

I was having fun with my friends and there were a few other kids from my class at school their too. It is really the only playground in town. Since we are a small town and there is only a limited number of hangouts for the primary school kids.

Matt was there with Peter, Sam, Alan, Adam and Jerry, who are some of the most popular boys in our class and my friends us girls are friends with the boys now this year, but only the ones that hang out with Matt. Who is there unannounced leader, like I am with the girls.

I mostly play with girls at school, although the boys do not tease us anymore in grade five and six like they did when we were younger and this year we play together sometimes. Besides I am starting to notice boys and so are my friends and we talk about crushes we have and so forth, although I haven't had my first kiss yet and neither have any of the other girls of my group. I am not sure who I like yet out of the boys and I am a bit young for that anyway. We are all just friends for now.

I was having fun with my friends and we were sitting on the playground and talking, but watching the boys too. They were running around the square next to the beach playing tag. Which is always fun.

Us girls decided to join the boys eventually playing tag. Running around the big square next to the beach. It's a great game and fun and an excuse to hang out with the cute popular boys from my class.

We got sick of tag eventually and were all on the playground. I was having my turn on the swing. I was taking a break and was just sitting on the swing and talking to my friend Matt. Who is one of the most popular boys in the class and we're starting to get along really well this year. Matt is a nice guy and we have known each other since were in grade prep, although we never got along until this year. Since Matt never used to play with girls, but now we get along ok and Matt is very popular at school and is the male school captain. I am the female school captain.

I got off the swing and my friends and I sat on the brick wall and the boys were in front of us and we were hanging out and having a lot of fun. I was sitting between Grace and Sophie, who are about my closest friends.

I was still sitting on the brick bench and was hanging out with my friends when Grace nudged me and said that we might have trouble. I looked up and nearly groaned, realising that Allison Ritz is heading straight for me and is not alone of course. She had Leanne Cummingo with her and several other girls from Liberty Grammar I am assuming and also several boys, including an Asian boy that looks similar to Allison. He might be her brother, although I haven't met him.

Well this is just great! What are those snobs doing here? I have not seen Allison Ritz since that huge argument we had at The Avenue. I was not happy to see her again or Leanne Cummingo either.

Great! I am not scared of the Liberty Grammar kids and don't care Allison is coming up to the bench. She is brave coming up considering the argument we had last time and also because I have a large group of friends there, but so does Allison.

Allison walked right up and recognised my friends and I straight away and walked right up to us. I took a look at Allison. She's really pretty and definitely looks Japanese with her long black hair and almond shaped eyes and she is a lot shorter than me. Which was amusing in the argument that we had. I am very tall for my age and tower over most of the girls in the class and the boys too sometimes, although mum told me that might change in high school.

Leanne was back too and Leanne's very pretty too and I think that she might be European. Since she has brown hair, brown eyes and olive skin. Both Allison and Leanne are in designer clothes. Skirts, sandals and singlet tops and dress similar I notice.

Allison knows me and just sauntered right up to me on the bench and gave me a dirty look and also Grace and Sophie looks, which I returned. Allison knows Grace and Sophie too from The Avenue.

I'm not scared of Allison and returned her look and asked what she wants and is doing here and Allison said that she's just hanging out with her friends like I am, but she also followed it up by saying that she is not happy to see me or my friends and what are we doing here?

Oh seriously! Who is this witch? Never leaving me alone. I told Allison that I'm just spending time with my friends and am not happy to see her either. I wasn't going to get into another argument with Allison after five minutes like last time and don't want to stoop to her level! Especially when I know that mum is not far and will be watching us. So I said to Allison to just leave it and asked who's with her and if her friends are from Liberty Grammar too and she said yes and looked surprised that I am talking to her. I had no interest in talking to Allison and Leanne, but want to avoid trouble because my mum is still at the café watching us and the last time I got into an argument with Allison my mum grounded me. I really don't need that!

Allison surprised me by not arguing with me either and

introduced her friends. I already know Leanne from The Avenue, but Allison said that the other girls are Ally, Laticia and Margaret and that the guys were her brother Aaron and Mitch.

I then introduced my friends. Grace, Sophie, Emma, Vicky, Amy and Charlotte and the boys came up and I said that this is Matt, Peter, Sam, Alan, Adam and Jerry.

Was it my imagination or did Aaron and Mitch look a bit nervous at all the boys that are with us? I wouldn't be surprised. Since they are outnumbered. Although Allison had her group there and I recognise those snobs as Liberty Grammar girls from the way that they are dressed and acting and at the moment they are not causing any trouble, but when Allison introduced her other friends, Leanne gave me a look and looked surprised and annoyed that Allison is talking to me.

Clearly this the popular group at Liberty Grammar and I know this anyway from my sister Monica. After my argument with Allison, Monica talked to me at length about the Liberty Grammar kids and who to watch out for. Especially next year when I start high school. Monica is just watching out for me and we are in the same school together next year, although Monica in year 11 and me in year 7. Monica said to watch out for Allison Ritz and Leanne Cummingo. They are trouble, even if they are my age and even the older girls have heard of them in my sisters year level.

. . .

So anyway I met Allison's friends and they weren't friendly, just said a stiff hello and I introduced my friends. I think that this needs to be done. I think or know from my older sister that Allison is considered a leader in the popular group at her school and so is her brother Aaron and I am considered a leader in my group at school. Considering that there has already been trouble between I'm getting the feeling that it's important to know who to watch out for at Liberty Grammar and I think that Allison is thinking the same thing.

I was talking to Allison, but not enjoying it. I think that this is important though. Everything was going fine for a little while when Leanne made a comment to Elise, calling her a tomboy. What the hell? My friend Elise is a bit of a tomboy. She plays basketball and is sportier then the rest of the group and doesn't usually dress in skirts or dresses, preferring jeans or tracksuit pants most of the time. We are really good friends though and I don't care. Elise is great and we grew up down the road from each other and are still really close.

So I did not appreciate what Leanne just called Elise! Neither did the rest of the group. Oh honestly, that Leanne Cummingo. She really is as bad as Allison and I have heard how Leanne is Allison's best friend and another leader in the popular crowd at Liberty Grammar.

I was proud of Elise and she didn't back away from Leanne and called her a snob. Oh no! I know from experience what Allison and Leanne are like in an argument and today I've got my whole group there and so do the Liberty Grammar kids. I wasn't upset with Elise for sticking up for herself to Leanne. Grace and Sophie were not that brave the other time at The Avenue when trouble happened last time.

Allison was not happy with Elise and asked her. What did you just call Leanne? Leanne was not happy either was shooting Elise dirty looks. Oh no!

I went up to see what was going on and so did Allison. I don't want an argument with my mum watching us at The Avenue, but if Allison starts one with me then I won't hesitate and will not back down from an argument.

I went up to Elise and asked what was going on and Allison went up to Leanne. Elise said that Leanne's just making comments and she doesn't know what her problem is. I then went up to Allison and Leanne and told Leanne to leave my friends alone and Leanne then commented that she just started the argument, Elise didn't back away from it.

I was starting to get annoyed and so were the Liberty Grammar kids. Especially when Allison called me a bimbo, again! Like the other night at The Avenue. Oh honestly! Who is this witch?

Of course Allison and I got into another argument after that. Not just us either, Allison's brother Aaron called Matt names that started an argument between the boys. Awesome!

Allison and I in an argument are as bad as each other. It is even amusing because we are both loud and stir each other up easily. It took exactly 10 minutes for an argument to break out! Honestly. This is ridiculous. I've seen Allison Ritz twice and already we are arguing like no tomorrow. I think that from the start we have just hated each other! That much is obvious.

Allison and I stopped our argument when I realised that my mum and Grace and Sophies mum were headed straight for us and don't look happy. Oh great! Don't tell me that Allison is getting me into trouble again! Like last time. This isn't making me like her any more. I stopped Arguing with Allison and so did my friends, but it was too late and mum could clearly hear us from the restaurant. I didn't know that I was that loud! Clearly I am though. Mum came over and told us to stop arguing and asked what happened. I told her and mum was still annoyed and said that we are going and so are my friends. We had plans to go to a movie anyway. The girls anyway. The boys are waiting on their parents.

As I went off with mum and my friends. I said bye to Matt, Peter, Sam, Alan, Adam and Jerry, but ignored Allison and her friends. My mum is not happy with me again and said that she's sick of this arguing and asked us girls what was going on. I was fuming as we walked off with Allison and knew that this won't be out only argument!

Part 3-Grade Six endings

Chapter 15

Stacey

I can't believe that I am graduating primary school in a few months and so are my friends. I just got back from spring holidays and so did my friends and it was really fun and I'm not looking forward to going back to school.

The school holidays were fun and I was in holiday care for nearly all of it and so were Robert, Shannon, David and Sabrina and nearly all of her friends. I didn't mind holiday care and it is fun. We do heaps of excursions and went out to the movies a couple of times and the trampoline park. We also went bowling. I don't know. Mum and dad still prefer me to be in after school care and holiday program until I start year 7 next year to be safe.

I am back at school now and starting term 4 in grade six. Which is a lot of pressure. All the kids in my class are in the same boat and everyone is talking about what school they are going to next year and I know that we will be getting split into two or even three schools for year 7.

I know that I will be moving on to Jefferson Secondary College next year and so will my friends Robert, Shannon and David. I decided that ages ago and it is easier to get to for high school because there is a short bus ride from my place or a 15 minute walk and my mum and dad can't drive me to school in the mornings due to work. It's easier going to that school then out to Rydal Secondary College in the other town. As that is nearly a half an hour bus ride.

It is an option for a lot of kids in my class though. Mainly the kids that are from the farms or don't mind travelling also because Rydal Secondary College is double the size of Jefferson Secondary College and has lots of available sports and activities.

It was also announced on Monday morning that the Liberty Grammar scholarships are going to be open again this year for any interested grade six students. For sport, music, and English, maths and art scholarships. One boy and one girl will be picked for each category and our school gets these opportunities every year.

Scholarships are a big deal and any kids picked are going to be officially announced at graduation and given awards. The scholarships are hard to get and for sports scholarships they base that on results, how well you do with the team and often it's the grade six captains for each sport picked, but not always.

Kids actually audition for music scholarships, which can be for dance, singing, or playing instruments and art is based on their current work and how they do with their classes.

English and maths scholarships are hard to get and you need to pass the exams to get into Liberty Grammar. The scholarships are given out at the end of the year and announced at graduation.

I am not going for any of the scholarships and have no interest in going to school at Liberty Grammar to be with all of those snobs. Neither do my friends. I have heard that any kids on scholarship are not treated well and that the popular crowd can be mean. Which my friends from year 7 tell me. Although we all know from the way Allison and Leanne treat my friends and I and all of their friends and their older sisters.

So I am moving on the Jefferson Secondary College and am looking forward to starting high school next year.

End of primary school will be fun, as well worrying about graduating and results. We have a graduation, grade six dance and we will be going out for an excursion to an adventure park in a couple of weeks to celebrate the end of year too. Mum and dad also said that they would take me out to dinner after graduation.

…

On Saturday afternoon my mum drove me over to The Avenue with my friends Shannon, Robert and David. We want to go to the beach and mum offered to drive us and is meeting Shannon, Robert and David's mum's for lunch. They said that they'd drop us off at the beach and leave us to it for the first time. Which is exciting. Although I know that our mum's aren't far.

My mum and I were the first to arrive and sat on the brick wall that is next to the beach to wait for the others. It is a nice spot and faces The Avenue and the other side is right next to the beach, so it's fun to sit there and watch surfers and there is a playground, square and beachside cafes.

I talked to my mum and we get along really well. I get along well with both of my parents and am an only child. I always wanted a little brother or sister, but it hasn't happened. As a result my parents spoil me and always have.

The others were not long to arrive and Robert, Shannon, David were there with their mums and loaded down with beach gear. My mum is going out to lunch with the other mum's and I am going to the beach with my friends. Then we are all going to a movie. My mum is very close to the other mum's. Particularly Shannon and Robert's mum's and is good friends with David's mum too since their family moved to town.

My mum grew up with Shannon and Robert's mum's and my mum has lived in my hometown her whole life, although my dad lived in Brisbane until he married my mum. My mum has been friends with Robert and Shannon's mum's since they were five years old and in primary school! Which is cute and they are still best friends to this day. David's mum came into the picture when we became friends with David and she's also very close to my mum and Robert's and Shannon.

I love Shannon and Robert's mums! Their dad's too. Their mums are like aunties to me and I grew up going to Shannon and Robert's houses from when I was a baby and I love both their families. Robert's mum spoilt me rotten as a kid and Shannon too and adored us like we were the daughters she never had and we are still both very close to Robert's mum. Shannon's mum too. We grew up going to her house and both of them used to babysit us when we were little and my mum and dad babysat Robert and Shannon too.

Our dads are all really close too. Actually my dad is out with Robert, Shannon and David's dad's today! They are all playing golf and my dad enjoys golf and goes out to play golf every couple of weeks, usually with my friends dad's as my mum doesn't enjoy golf. My dad is sporty and I take after him in that regard. He used to play basketball and still plays golf, goes to the gym a lot and plays tennis with my mum too.

...

Anyway! Everyone had arrive and said hi and mum said hi to all the mums and to Robert, Shannon and David too and gave my friends a big hug! Mum adores my friends and my friends like my mum too. I got a big from Shannon, Robert and David's mums. They said how tall I've gotten and that I am getting pretty. I like all their mums and they are almost like aunties to me.

After everyone said hi I headed down to the beach with my friends after our mum's made sure we had everything and knew to contact them if we get into trouble. I know that they are just worried, but we'll be fine. I know this beach well and so do my friends and it's only a couple of hours and then we are all going to the movies.

I walked down to the beach and talked to Robert and Shannon and David are in front of us and are talking lively. Shannon and David get along great and are really good friends and I am too with David. He is a great guy and so is Robert and our group is really close.

I was disappointed that Anna couldn't come to the beach today. I wanted Anna to come since we are good friends and Anna is joining us for school next year, although at the moment she goes to Rydal primary school. Anna and I play basketball together and are close, but she could not make it today.

I was having fun with my friends and Robert and David were joking around with Shannon and I. We all like the beach and I have enjoyed it since I was little and my parents are always taking me to the beach and my friends too.

We have a beach right in town which is very convenient and only about 15 walk from my house and it is a surf beach that is popular with everyone in town and also tourists since there is great scenery too.

I have always loved the beach and my parents have had me in swimming lessons in both pool and beach since I was a baby since they wanted me to be safe in the surf beaches and I think I might take up surfing the next couple of years, but we will see.

I walked down to the beach with my friends and we laid our towels out and I took my shorts and t-shirt off and had a blue one piece on and I had sunglasses on and thongs and laid out my towel and already had sunscreen on from when I was at home and will top it up later. I have very fair skin and it burns easily. So I have to be careful in the sun. I also had a hat on. Shannon had a one piece on and the boys were in board shorts and we had an umbrella too and thankfully Robert and David are tall enough to set it up, although it was a challenge without our parents too help. We had also brought plenty of food. I went with mum to get some snacks, including chips, some chocolate drinks and some sandwiches that we made. My friends had brought stuff too for lunch.

I lay my towel out next to Shannon on one side and Robert on the other and David was next to Shannon. I lay back and sun-baked and talked to my friends. We were having fun and at this time of the day beach wasn't that crowded, which is good.

We were having fun and were talking and sunbaking and had something to eat. Eating lunch and snacking out. We went for a swim after lunch making sure not to go right after lunch and I just jumped right in and jumped over waves and wasn't scared being in a surf beach and neither are my friends. We all like the beach and have been in swimming lessons for years.

I was having fun with my friends and splashed their faces and we had a good long session swimming and then went back up to the beach and had some more food and sun backed.

Mum called as I was sun backing to remind me the movie is starting in an hour and that we had better look at getting ready.

Mum was right and I am looking forward to the movie and so are my friends. The cinema isn't far from us and they have a shower block and toilets at the top of the beach and I had brought a change of clothes. Our mum's are meeting us up at The Avenue. We packed up all the food and tent and our towels and headed up to The Avenue and my mum, Robert's, Shannon's and David were there waiting for us and I gave mum my beach stuff to put in the car while I have a shower and so did my friends. I went to the girl's change room with Shannon and we talked a bit about how much fun we had at the beach and how nice it was being trusted like that. I hope that I get to do that again!

We aren't going to the movie on our own though and are all going in a group with our mum's. I had a shower and dried my blond hair with a towel and changed into some jeans, a blue t-shirt and some sandals and tied my hair back in a ponytail. I grabbed my bag and Shannon and I hung out and talked while we got ready.

We didn't take long and met the boys and our mum's outside and helped our mum's put the bags in the car. I headed out to the movies with everyone. Feeling great how the day had gone.

Chapter 16

Grade six Jefferson Primary graduation

Stacey

On Friday morning I woke up with a feeling of excitement knowing that today is my graduation. Today we have the graduation ceremony at school and a full day ahead of the ceremony and then we have dinner and a party afterwards, which is something that we are all looking forward to. It will be our first school dance.

On Friday afternoon I put on the dress that my mum helped me buy and my first pair of heels. Although they were not too high. I was not happy about wearing a dress, but I had to for graduation. It is formal and all the other girls will be wearing dresses or skirts and the boys will all be dressed up too.

The dress was knee length and red and had short sleeves, but was not too low cut, my parents would not let me wear anything not age appropriate.

I am not happy about being in a dress anyway and do not really take notice of what I look like. I have grown though and am getting tall already. Everyone has noticed that, and I am around 5'6 now and taller than most of the girls in my class and a lot of the boys too and certainly Shannon! She is much shorter than me. I hope that I do not get much taller, although my parents both think that I will. As both my mum and dad are very tall and so are my aunties on mum's side.

I do not know. I am 12 years old and hit my growth spurt this year and am still growing, although it is slowing down a bit according to my parents. Shannon is short at 5'0 and Robert is taller than me at 5'8 already and David towers over our whole group and is 5'10 already.

I do not know! We will see how tall I get and in some ways being tall is good. It helps me with basketball. I have long legs too and am already developed more than I like and am curvy with small breasts and got my period this year.
I put on the dress and shoes and brushed out my blond hair. I have shoulder length blond hair and blue eyes and usually just tie my hair back into a ponytail, but tonight I kept it hanging loose. I did not put makeup on. My dad does not want me to wear it yet and I do not want to wear it anyway. I think I will wait until high school and then for school functions.

I was finally ready and went downstairs to my parents and they said that I looked gorgeous and could not believe that I am graduating today. We are driving over to school and graduation will be several hours before dinner and the school disco. My parents are not invited to that. Since it is our first school dance and teachers are chaperoning the dance.
I drove over to the school with my parents, who were also dressed up and dad found a park in the car park, and I

walked out with my parents and found Robert and Shannon in front of school with David and all four sets of parents. Robert's brother Sal was also there and David's brother Shane. We said hi to everyone and so did my parents.

Shannon looked pretty and had a blue knee length dress on with short heels like me and like me also was not wearing makeup, although she had added some earrings and a bracelet. I had on a necklace my parents gave me and earrings too.

Shannon said a lively hello and looked excited and so did Robert. I was shell shocked looking at Robert and could not believe how cute my guy best friend is all dressed up and David looked cute too. Although I would not tell them that! That would be awkward.

Robert was wearing an outfit I am sure his parents would have forced him into, although he looked handsome and older than 12 years old. Robert was wearing black pants, a blue shirt and even a tie, but all the boys are encouraged to dress up for graduation and so are the girls. David is also in dress pants, a shirt and dress shoes and looks older than 12 years old like Robert.

My mum took a photo of Robert, Shannon David and I and so did Robert, Shannon, and David's parents. My mum said that Robert and I look cute, all dressed and so do Shannon and David. I was having fun with my friends' taking photos outside the hall and my parents had a few shots with me as well.

We had gotten our graduation outfits by then. Our teacher came out and gathered us up to go inside and my parents went in and sat down and were in the audience, but I am not sitting with them. I will be sitting up the front with my classmates.

I walked in with my friends and said hi to the other kids in my class and could see Sabrina Brewer and her friends standing with the popular boys. Sabrina is in a dress and has makeup on. Her parents allowed it for graduation and looks gorgeous with her blond hair, blue eyes, and long legs. Sabrina said hi to us and so did her friends and we stood with the class and our teacher organized us into a line according to our surnames. As we are sitting like that to be able to get our diplomas in order.

Our school is not overly large, but there are quite a few grade six students graduating. The principle is planning to hand out awards, announce the scholarship winners and then do all the diplomas one by one for all the students. So, we will be here for a while. I was seated nowhere near Robert or Shannon. Since seating is done by surname. I was seated between Vicky on one side and Jerry on the other and I know them, although not too well. We talked a bit. They are both part of Sabrina and Matts group at school and are in my class.

Once everyone was seated the principal came out to make the speech, which the rest of our teachers are sitting in a couple of rows behind us students and can keep an eye on us from where they are, and our families and friends are behind the teachers. The principle and vice principle are up on stage.

The principal made a long speech congratulating this year's graduates and wishing the grade six class good luck for high school and thanked the teachers and everyone that came. The principal then said that he has some important awards to hand out and scholarship winners to announce.

So, the English and math's awards went to Sierra and Mitch. Who are two of the smartest kids in the class and did get the highest grades for the English and math's tests. The principle also announced that Sierra was the English scholarship winner and would be attending Liberty Grammar next year for high school. Mitch had not made the scholarship for math's although he got great grades. Mitch did not go for the scholarship at all because he did not want it and said that in class.

Not all kids want to go to Liberty Grammar and only some go for the scholarship. Clearly Sierra is one of them and is about to become a Liberty Grammar girl and likely to be blacklisted from friends from Jefferson Secondary College when she does. Since the schools do not get along. I do not know Sierra well. She is in a different class to mine, although I know her by name and so do my friends. She is part of Sabrina Brewers group, but not one of her close friends. This will be interesting! I know that and do not know how Sabrina will react to Sierra getting into Liberty Grammar. We will see, but it does not affect me.

Mitch is a nice guy. Quiet and not part of the main popular group. He will have a talk with my friends and I when we see him. Sierra and Mitch sat down, and they got their diplomas with their certificates, all the awards winners were first and then the rest of us.

Next up were the art awards and music. Which went to Annie and Melanie. They would be going to Liberty Grammar too, along with Sierra, surprisingly. Anna and Melanie are quite girls that are not part of the popular group and incredibly talented at art and music. They went and collected their awards and diplomas So that is three scholarships now! All girls too, although the sports ones are coming up and they are usually extremely competitive. The boy's art and music scholarships also went to Rydal primary school.

Drama and dance also went to Rydall primary school as the best dance and drama kids in our class are Sabrina Brewer and her friends. Sabrina would have won the dance scholarship if she had gone for it, but no way would that happen! Sabrina Brewer at Liberty Grammar in Allison and Leanne's class next year. Sabrina's going to Jefferson Secondary College and so are her friends Emma, Vicky, and Charlotte. We will be in the same year level for high school next year.

Liberty Grammar offers scholarships for sport too and usually one for a boy and a girl in each sport except rugby and netball. The rugby scholarship is for a boy this year and the netball is for a girl until they bring in a girl's rugby team. We are currently looking at that now, but not enough girls signed up this year for rugby and none of the boys play netball. Since there is only a girls' team.

I did not go for any of the sports scholarships and neither did my friends, although I knew that it was possible to get the swimming or basketball scholarship for me. My coaches said that I could go for those scholarships, but I have no interest in going to Liberty Grammar and going to school with those complete snobs and neither do my friends.

There was a bit of a disagreement with my parents over that and I knew that my mum and dad would have liked me to go for a scholarship, but thankfully I have parents that don't force me to do something I don't want to do and after my fight with Leanne mum kind of understands I could be in trouble there and so does dad. I want to go to high school with Shannon, Robert, and David anyway next year. It would be awful if I were separated from my best friends.

To my great surprise I heard my name called for the girls' basketball award for grade six and was thrilled and I could see my parents at the back going crazy and clapping like mad and so were my friends. It was a surprise and a proud moment for me since I am not particularly academic, although I love sport. I also got a special award that goes to one boy and one girl for best all-around athlete for grade six.

I could not believe it! This was a huge honor and an incredibly special award that means that you have had impressive results in sport throughout your primary school years and particularly in grade six. I went up to collect my awards and diploma and mum came up to take a photo of me and looked proud and so did dad.

I sat back down reeling and I knew that the basketball scholarship ended up going to another Rydal kid since I turned it down. The boys' basketball award went to Matt, which is not a surprise, he is team captain and my counterpart on the boys' team.

Matt was also the boys all round athlete award, on top of my friends Robert and David, which was crap. They are also great athletes, but Matt is on the basketball team, swim team and does athletics too. I took the girl's award, but Shannon did not, although she is very sporty too.

Shannon, Robert, and David all got sports awards but. Shannon for netball, Robert for soccer and David for Rugby and the girls' soccer award went to Elise from Sabrina Brewer's group. Since she could not get the basketball award because I got the basketball award I am assuming. Since Elise is also a sports star at the school. Elise is a real athlete too. She plays basketball, soccer and does athletics. Elise is a great basketball player, but she is also great at soccer. Only one award was for each category.

Most of the scholarships were turned down by the awards winners but, which is amusing. None of my friends want to go to Liberty Grammar and neither do the popular kids. They want to go to the public schools together next year. Either Jefferson Secondary or Rydall Secondary, which is a lot better in the popular group than Liberty Grammar.

The sports scholarships went to Alexa, who took the swimming award for the girls and accepted the scholarship to Liberty Grammar. My competition on the team! Alexa was going to Liberty Grammar. I could not believe it. The basketball scholarship went to Isac. Matt's vice-captain on the team and they do not get along. Isac's never been part of the popular group, another girl got soccer from Rydal Secondary College, since no one went to it from our school.

I cannot believe Alexa is going to Liberty Grammar! I am in shock. Alexa and I have been swimming teammates and friends since we were five years old and Alex is a great swimmer, but now she is going to Liberty Grammar. I just know how the scholarship kids are treated there and hope that Alexa will be ok, that is the reason I did not want the scholarship.

The boy's swimming award and scholarship went to Alex and the boy's athletics scholarship winner went to Gary and he got the award also and the girl's athletics award went to Christy. The final award was for dance, and no one was surprised at Sabrina Brewer taking out that award considering she has been dancing since before primary school. Sabrina did not take the dance scholarship though. To the surprise of no-one! There is no way Sabrina's going to school at Liberty Grammar next year. With how much she hates Allison and Leanne especially.

The dance scholarship went to Missy. Who is another girl in our class that is Sabrina's main competition in dance competitions at school and outside of school and they do not get along either.

There was a boy's dance scholarship winner too. Although not as many boys' dance at our school. The boy that won though is a bit of a star at dance and has been dancing as long as Sabrina and her friends have and is one of only 3 boys in Sabrina's competition team outside school. He has more female than male friends and gets along well with Sabrina and her friends and sometimes gets teased by the boys for dancing, although he does not care and enjoys it. Drama went to Rydall Secondary College kids for scholarships and Emma from Sabrina's group got the drama award for the girls and Adam for the boys. They both turned the scholarships down.

No-one was surprised when Shane got the dance award for the boy's and excepted the scholarship to Liberty Grammar. Although he will be blacklisted with Sabrina and her friends after accepting the scholarship. As we all know, Sierra from the group will be excluded from the group in high school, as no-one likes the Liberty Grammar kids. Sabrina and Matt also got a leadership award for being school captains this year.

So, they were the awards! That took a while and all the kids that won got congratulated, given their awards and then diplomas too and then the rest of the kids in the grade got their diplomas one by one and it took a while, since there are quite a few kids in the class. The principal made another speech after the diplomas were finished. He thanked the teachers for grade six this year and the parents and then and mentioned some people by name.

...

Well graduation is over! I cannot believe it. It has gone so fast, and I am thrilled about my awards and so are my friends. We walked outside to meet with our parents and families. They had refreshments and drinks, and it was a wonderful day so most people were outside, although we could go inside if we wanted.

I stood outside with my friends and Robert, Shannon and David are as excited as I am, and we talked a mile a minute and ate snacks we got from the hall and had a lot of fun. Other friends came over too to hug us and talk a mile a minute and we spent time together with Sabrina and Matt's group a bit.

My parents had come out and so did Robert, Shannon and David and both gave me a hug and said how proud they are of me and we had a family photo with me in my graduation gown and I still had the dress and heels on and then we had a big group shot with Robert, Shannon and David's parents and Robert's little brother Sal, David's brother Shane and then just hung out a bit outside the hall. We were not there for long though. As my parents were going to take me out for some ice cream and coffee to celebrate graduation. Since the school disco is on tonight, which is just for us kids, with teachers supervising.

I headed out with my parents and said goodbye to my friends. We just wanted to have a bit of family time and they were going to drop me back off at school in a few hours.

We went to a beachside café that I like, and so did my parents and mum and dad get coffees and ice cream and I got ice cream and lemonade. It was fun and a nice café and a lot of kids from graduation were there too, since it is a popular café.

I stayed there for a bit with my parents and then went for a walk down The Avenue with them. Which is always fun.

Then we headed home. There are still a couple of hours to go before the disco.

I headed home and just stayed in my dress and heels, since I am wearing those tonight and do not want to get changed again, although I am dying to get into tracksuit pants! Trust me, but the disco is dressy. I watched some television, relaxed a bit, headed out after a while, and got picked up by Robert's mum. She is giving Robert, Shannon, and I a lift to the disco and I am looking forward to tonight.

Chapter 17

Sabrina

I am looking forward to my first school disco tonight and so are my friends. Graduation is over and it was long, and boring, although I got a leadership award and an award for dance which is exciting. I did not take the scholarship that was awarded to the winner and neither did most of my friends. I have no desire to go to school at Liberty Grammar with those stupid snobs, although I am happy that I won the award. I still cannot believe that Sierra took the Liberty Grammar scholarship and so did Shane. Who are both friends of mine.

No-one is happy with Sierra right now! From my group or Shane. As they took the scholarships and Matt and I have already decided that anyone that takes the Liberty Grammar scholarships will no longer be part of our group in high school. Due to Allison and Leanne and their company at that school becoming worse and worse this year and tensions between our school are not getting any better, in fact they are getting worse.

I do not care if my friends in the group are going to Rydal Secondary College. I know that Elise, Grace, and Sophie are going to that school next year and not Jefferson Secondary College and so are the boys Alan and Jerry.

I am fine with my friends who go to Rydal Secondary College, although I will miss them. Especially Elise, Grace, and Sophie. I know, and so do my friends, that it is not anyone's fault if you must change schools in high school. I know that my friends are expected to, and their parents want them to change and at least it is another public school! Not Liberty Grammar.

I think that as much as I hate it, I am going to give a talk to Allison Ritz at some point about high school and how things are going to work next year between our schools. I am the leader of the girls of my group and Allison is the ringleader of the Liberty Grammar girls and this year there has already been trouble between our groups. At the playground and when I first met Allison and Leanne at The Avenue.
I do not know what to do about the situation or how to protect my friends. Particularly Emma, Vicky, Amy, and Charlotte. Who are coming to Jefferson Secondary College with me. I do know that I personally cannot stand that Allison Ritz or any of her friends and am getting sick of her picking on my friends and I whenever she gets the chance.

I have even talked to Matt about the situation and know that out of the boys only Matt, Peter and Sam are coming to Jefferson Secondary College. Matt also said we need to watch out for Liberty Grammar kids too and I know from my older sister Monica too as she has had a lot of problems with girls from that school too.

We will see what happens, but I just want to enjoy tonight and so do my friends. I am looking forward to my first school dance and the girls of my group have been talking about it all week and what we are going to wear and so forth and said that if any of the boy's ask us to dance, we will dance with them if they are from our group, but I do not know about that!

I got dressed back into the blue dress I wore for graduation, although I have been home for a few hours and got changed when I got home to be comfortable. I love my new dress and it is knee length and has short sleeves and I wore my first high heels with them, but not too high and have a matching black handbag. Mum is letting me wear makeup too today, but not too much. So, I had some lipstick and foundation on and a bit of eyeshadow. I also put on a bracelet and some earrings, with a necklace.

I was ready to go! My mum was giving me a lift over to the school hall with Grace and Sophie. My other friends are meeting us at the dance. Grace and Sophie live around the corner from me, although they are moving to the other town soon and changing schools next year as their dad just got a new job in the other town. We are all really upset about this! Grace and Sophie are two of my best friends.

Mum picked up Grace and Sophie and their mum came out and said hi to mum. Since they are friends too. Grace and Sophie got into the backseat and said hi to me and my mum and they both had dresses and makeup and heels on too and looked good.

We drove over the hall and the school dance is being held in the hall where we usually have functions, assembly's and graduation was here earlier too and the teachers would have been busy setting up this afternoon, which is why we were told to go home for a few hours. My parents dropped me off and into the hall and made sure that Grace, Sophie, and I had found our friends and table before they left.

I was fine and the teachers took us to the table, and we got to pick who we were sitting with. So, I had Elise, Grace, Sophie, Vicky, Amy, and Charlotte and that is who I picked, and Sierra is on the same table and Alexa, Karen, and Missy.

I was not too happy with my table right now and unfortunately the teachers had us pick a week ago, before the graduation and that is who I hand around out of the girls at school normally, although now that I think about it, I should have asked Stacey and Shannon or the boys to sit with us instead of Sierra, Alexa, and Missy.

I am not happy with Sierra, Alexa and Missy and am the unannounced leader of the group, so my friends follow what I do most of the time, although we are all good friends.

Sierra took the scholarship at Liberty Grammar and so did Shane. Sierra therefore is blacklisted from my group next year and so is Shane. Sierra took the scholarship given by Liberty Grammar and is about to become a Liberty

Grammar girl. To the disbelief of my entire group. Alexa and Missy are Sierra's best friends and are moving to Rydall Secondary College next year. Missy and Alex are making it clear whose side they are on, and it is not mine. They are sticking with Sierra and Shane and do not want to stop talking to them. They told me that this afternoon when we nearly got into an argument outside the hall our parents dispersed quickly. So now Sierra, Missy and Alex are sitting at my table tonight! That is awkward. There is already tension on the table and within my group.

Anyway! What can you do? I will leave it for tonight and just want to have fun. The boys are sitting at the table next to us. Matt, Peter, Sam, Alan, Adam and Jerry and they have Mitch, Gary, Shane, and Alex too and we decided to separate the boys and girls when picking tables and Matt and I decided that and dictated who sits with us tonight and again out of the boys. Shane also took a Liberty Grammar scholarship.

I particularly cannot believe Shane took the dance scholarship at Liberty Grammar and am as upset about that as Sierra, Missy, and Alexa. I like Shane and so do my friends and we have been friends for years. Shane dances in the same troop I do and competes with it and is close to all us girls and feels like one the girls most of the time! Which is funny, but Shane taking the scholarship makes him as bad as my other friends who took the scholarship.

I was having fun with my friends and said hi to people and we are having dinner at the dance, which is why there are tables set up. We ate pasta, garlic bread and meat with salad and for dessert there was cake made by cooks at the school. Everyone was eating, even the teachers and they had their own table and looked like they were having fun. They are chaperoning the dance and our parents are not here tonight.

I talked to my friends, and we ate, talked, and drank soft drinks and punch. I was thoroughly full after that! I really was and so were my friends.
It was fun at the dance and after dinner the music started up and one of the teachers acted as Disk jockey and put up a song that everyone likes and asked for some requests. I was one of the first to get up to dance. I love dancing and so do my friends and Emma, Vicky, Amy, and Charlotte were quick to join me.

It was fun dancing, and they had a good variety of music. There were more kids dancing, mostly girls and Matt and the popular boys were not dancing yet, although Shane was dancing with Sierra, Missy, and Alexa.

They played a slow song after that. Which was amusing, but it is a good song that we all like and I was not sure how to dance to this one, unless we are dancing with boys and my friends, and I were standing in a group on the side of the dance floor talking and watching Matt and the boys who were over talking by the punch bowl and food by now but are watching us girls too.
We are all only 12 years old, but I am open to dancing with one of the boys if they ask and so are my friends and we talked about that before the dance.
 Well, someone had to make the first move. I was surprised when Adam came up to ask me to dance and I

was the first girl to be asked to do the slow dance in the whole place. What a bragging point. Adam is cute and I had no issues dancing with him and we are friends.

Matt asked Emma to dance shortly after and Vicky, Amy and Charlotte danced with Peter, Sam, and Jerry. So that is the whole group, and we are the first kids brave enough to dance together out of the boys and girls and we are all part of the same group anyway. It was fun dancing with Adam, and we did not get too close, although I put my arms around his neck, and he had them on my waist as it is a slow song. We talked a bit and had two dances and then they played some faster songs, although I could see a few kids dancing together during the slow songs. What a night it has been so far! I am having heaps of fun and so are my friends.

Chapter 18

Stacey

I had just arrived at the school dance and found my table easily and was of course sitting with Shannon, Robert and David and a bunch of other kids from grade six at school, but none of Sabrina or Matt's group of friends.

Sabrina is regretting that decision now after graduation and we were not allowed to sit at the popular kids table as Shannon and I wanted to sit with Robert and David and the popular boys are sitting with the other boys on a separate table and Robert and David do not want to sit at that table because they do not have a good relationship with some of those boys, especially Peter, Sam, and Matt.

Sierra and Alexa are brave to be at that table and so is Shane on the boys' table, after they took the Liberty Grammar scholarships. Sabrina is not happy either about having them sit there, although they have no choice now.

I was happy with my table and did not care about sitting with the popular girls, particularly since increasingly Sabrina Brewer has been taking more control of the group.

...

Anyway! Enough on that. My friends and I made a lively table, and the food was delicious and so were the drinks and when the music started playing, I did not get up to dance straight away. I do not like dancing, except for fun. Unlike Sabrina and her friends. Who got on the dance floor straight away and are showing off, which is not surprising. Sabrina, Emma, Vicky, and Charlotte all dance competitively and so does Shane. The girls Sierra and Alexa and Missy joined them too.

Shane amuses my friends and me. He is a nice guy but prefers girls for friends and is as competitive with dancing as Sabrina and her friends. Shane is very girly in a lot of ways and does not enjoy sport.

I talked to Shannon and Robert, who are either side of me and we were having a lot of fun at the dance and the music was good, the teacher that was acting Disc jockey got requests from everyone and played some popular songs and a couple of slow songs, which was quite funny. Aren't we a bit young for slow dancing? Although I could see a few boys and girls dancing together, mostly Sabrina and Matts group.

I was quite surprised when Robert asked me to dance, and Shannon got asked by David. I had no issues dancing with

Robert. Since we are such good friends, it is fun to join in on the dance. I danced with Robert, although we did not get too close and more like in a waltz position and talked. To the next song I danced with David and Shannon danced with Robert this time.

After the dances they played lots more fun songs, and it was a great night and over much too quickly! My parents came to pick me up and the teachers cleaned up, so we did not have to stick around. I said bye to my friends and headed off. It had been a great night!
Liberty Grammar Graduation
Chapter 19
Leanne
On Friday morning I woke up and started getting ready for graduation, which is starting soon. It is an important day for me, and my friends and we are all excited and there is going to be a graduation party at a reception for all the families of the grade six graduates.

There are two graduations happening today, one for grade sixes and the year 12's has their graduation today too, although their graduation will be held separate from ours. My parents are excited for me and are coming to graduation of course and so is my older sister Marie and then to the party afterwards and said that they are proud of me.

I got dressed in a black dress that my parents bought for me, and I love it! It is knee length, with spaghetti straps and I brought my first pair of high heels to go with the dress, too although they are not too high, and mum took me to get my hair done professionally and it is half up with soft curls looks great! I am happy with the way I have my hair and for the first time I am wearing makeup too for graduation and have some lipstick foundation and eyeshadow and I added a bracelet, some earrings, and a necklace.

I am meeting my friends at the school for graduation, and we are all going with our parents, and I am looking forward to the party tonight, although graduation might be a bit boring.

I was ready to go and left with my parents and sister Marie and I got into the small limousine that my parents owned and we have a family driver as a wealthy family. I like having a chauffeur. It really is a statement as to my family's wealth and my friend Allison totally agrees with that too.

We got over to Liberty Grammar and got dropped off in front of the school and my parents left me with my friends, as my parents will be going inside to sit with the other parents and families and so is my older sister Marie. Marie is talking to her friends anyway and some of them are also older siblings of my friends. I stood outside the hall with my class and said hi to Allison and her brother Aaron, who are both in my class, and Ally, Laticia, and Monica, some of my best friends at school and Aaron had a few of his friends there too. His best friend Mitch is there and Steve, Aaden, and Michael. This is my group at school, and we are all close, even with the boys now. As we are all getting older, we spend time together at school and are considered the popular group.

Allison said hi to me and so did my other friends and we had all tried to dress up for graduation. We are expected to anyway and Allison said she would like all us girls to wear dresses and I am wearing low heels for the first time and so are my friends and makeup, which before today I did not wear.

Allison said hi to me and so did my other friends and we had all tried to dress up for graduation. We are expected to anyway and Allison said she would like all us girls to wear dresses and I am wearing low heels for the first time and so are my friends and makeup, which before today I did not wear.

I was having fun with my friends and the teachers were frantic, getting us organized and in lines according to our surname and I was right near the front and nowhere near Allison due to my last name Cummingo. We were lining up to go into the hall and sit down and already got given our graduation gowns and robes to put over our clothes. The teachers are doing this the proper way! Although at our school graduation is important, even in grade six and means you are moving to the big school next year.

We also know that some students from Jefferson primary school will be at graduation so that the principal can announce the scholarship winners from Jefferson primary school and Rydal primary school that are coming to our school next year for high school.
This annoys my friends and I and my parents, although there are scholarship kids every year and only for high school kids. Scholarships are for year 7 kids and that is the

only year they are allowed to apply to our school and do the exams and tests to get in. Scholarship kids are not treated well at my school, which is why I know some kids do not take scholarships. None of my friends are going to come from Jefferson primary school or Rydall primary school or any of the other popular kids and it is like that in the high school. The scholarship kids usually stick together and are teased by the popular kids in my sister's year. I am going to follow the same thing next year.

I do know at least that Sabrina Brewer and Stacey Green are not coming to our school next year or any of their friends. Thankfully, Stacey and Sabrina are at our school! No thanks. I cannot stand those idiots, neither can my friends. Allison and I have talked quite a bit about Stacey Green since my fight with her. Allison said quite frankly that she is surprised that Sabrina has not officially done anything with Stacey Green or tried to get her to join the popular group. I agree with Allison and think that Stacey is one to watch out for in high school and is trouble. She is also tall, with blond hair, blue eyes and legs that run for days, and I think she might be popular at Jefferson Secondary College.

Stacey is not part of Sabrina's group but, at least not yet and Stacey is quiet and shy and hangs out with boys and Shannon Chambers, but she is also tough in a fight, hates Allison and I and our friends and is as tall and blond as Sabrina Brewer. Sabrina is another story to Stacey and Allison knows that Sabrina at least is moving to Jefferson Secondary College with some of her closest friends. Sabrina is the ringleader of that group and trouble for my friends and me. I can tell already.

We are just too different and frankly no one thinks that kids that cannot pay their way should be coming to our school. My parents think that and often say that they pay thousands to send Marie and I to school. This is how many parents at my school feel about scholarship kids and my friends and I agree, and Allison particularly has said that next year we will not be letting any scholarship kids into our group when they come to our school for year 7, especially if they come from Jefferson Secondary College. Allison Ritz is slowly taking over my group at school and so is her brother Aaron. Allison is a natural leader and is extremely popular and well liked at school and admired for her big house, wealthy parents, dress sense and having a cool older cousin Lara and her mum is very glamourous and well dressed and her dad is wealthy and respected. They own two shopping malls and property and are the wealthiest family in town.

Allison is a natural leader and oversees the girls in the group and her brother Aaron is just as popular as Allison and everyone likes Aaron and wants to hang out with him and he is great at a sport, is good looking and has lots of friends. The guys all listen to what Aaron says. Aaron and Allison are close and are best friends as well as siblings. This helps them a lot at school.

Aaron and Allison are powerful at my school and extremely popular and work together to run the popular group and we are becoming the same group this year. With the boys and girls in my class. At Liberty Grammar it is all about prestige money, what your parents do for a living and how you look and dress to get into the popular group and Allison's got it. She is one of the best-looking girls in school and being Asian works in Allison's favor. The guys love her looks and Allison looks different to the rest of my friends and I. Allison and Aarons family, including their cousin Lara are the only Asian family in my town.

Neither Allison or Aaron like public school kids and neither do I or anyone in my group and I particularly hate that witch Stacey Green and all her friends, especially Shannon and Robert. I also do not like Sabrina Brewer and company. Her entire group is so annoying and Sabrina and Allison have a fiery relationship and I know that Sabrina is a leader at her school, like Allison is at ours and thankfully none of those idiots are taking scholarships at our school next year and Allison said that she would rather have anyone take a scholarship then Sabrina Brewer, but Sabrina would not do that anyway because she hates us and anyone at our school and so does her entire group at Jefferson primary school.

…

Anyway, enough on that. I sat down between my friend Ally and had Daniel on my other side. Who is in another class, but he is a nice guy, and I was talking to Ally and Daniel. I like Ally. We are good friends at school, and she is part of our main group.

Once the principal got on stage we stopped talking and listened to his speeches and announcements and he first announced the scholarship winners from Jefferson and Rydal Secondary College. He is doing our school rewards and graduation certificates after that.

The scholarship winners from Jefferson primary school were announced and so were the Rydall primary school winners for each category. Scholarships are important at our school and are offered every year in English and math's, rugby, swimming, basketball, soccer, athletics, netball, and music, art, dance, and drama. So, it took a while to get all the awards out and the scholarship winners were announced, given awards and certificates and all sat together near the front. They were especially invited to graduation and are expected to stay and are even invited to the reception tonight like my friends and I are.

There was a surprising number of winners from Rydal primary too, which happens rarely. Only if Ivory Grammar can't take them, or no-one takes the scholarships from Jefferson Secondary College. I don't mind though. The less Jefferson primary idiots at our school the better. Rydal primary is another school in the other town and none of us know them too well at Liberty Grammar. For the most part they go to Ivory Grammar for scholarships. The other local private school in the other town. Ivory Grammar and our school Liberty Grammar know each other as we compete often for sport and academics, but we are very competitive and don't particularly get along, although we respect kids from there before the public schools.

Amy got the scholarship for basketball, netball was Machelle, soccer was Alan and Amanda, Michael, Athletics, arts Adam, Alana maths and Mike and Daniel is music. They are all Rydal Secondary and joined the Jefferson primary school scholarship kids and the principle congratulated all of them and said welcome to Liberty

Grammar. Scholarships are always a big deal at our school! Trust me. They do this every year and kids need to be stars to get those scholarships and don't need to pay to go to our high school next year.

Those kids sat down and usually with their parents, since they are guests today and not from our school yet and had their own graduation at their school.

The principle did our school awards next and no no-ones getting a scholarship from our school! Since paying Liberty Grammar kids families are usually wealthy and can afford the fees. Awards are a big deal at my school and made much of and at the end of grade six all of us were given tests before we enter high school for each subject to see where we are at academically. It gives our high school teachers an idea of areas we need to improve or have help on next year. Although my friends and I hate those tests! Why did we have to have an exam in grade six? We'll have to have enough of those next year.

Liberty Grammar is a strict private school though and we are expected to work hard with schoolwork and teachers can be strict with us. I do not like school and neither do my friends and I just like hanging out with my friends. I do not think I will win any awards, but we will see.

The English award went to Melanie, which was no surprise to my friends and I. Melanie is smart and quiet and scared of my group! Since Allison and I tease her. The maths award went to Scott. Science was Misty, music went to Dennis, art to Alan, dance to Amanda, who is going to be competition for Missy, she is a great dancer at our school and none of the boys won dance, the rugby awards were Danielle and Mitch. A boy and a girl, since we have two teams at our school, Soccer was Aaden and Laticia, and basketball finally was Samantha and Dave. Allison got the leadership award for being school captain for grade six this year and so did Mitch, the male school captain.

I did not get any awards and was not expecting to. I am not that great at school. I am not into sports and do not do any music or dance classes either. I am a child model, or at least pre-teen anyway and have been doing catalogue shoots and commercials since I was a little girl and I also do beauty pageants when they are on. I usually go to Brisbane for beauty pageants though and I enjoy them, but I want to break into modelling and do a lot more of that in high school and gain some runway experience when I am old enough. My mum has had me doing all this kind of stuff since I was a little girl and I still enjoy it, but there are no school awards for that kind of work.

Everyone got their awards and diplomas, and the principle made more speeches and congratulated all the grade six graduates and then we were free! We went outside to our parents and families and my parents took a bunch of photos of me in my graduation gown and of my friends too and we had a large group shot.

There is a graduation party tonight, but we have a couple of hours to do what we want, and the party is being held at a reception centre and will be mixed with the year 12 graduates and we grade six graduates. My sister Marie is happy about that! Since all the cute year 12 boys will be there and some of her older high school friends and Marie is glad that there will be kids her age and older there. I will not see much of my sister tonight and I know it, although Marie and I get along well, but my sister is a teenager that loves hanging out with her friends and will be trying to talk to the year 12 boys and hang out with the older teenagers at the party and they might let her. Since Monica is extremely popular at the school and knows some of the year 12 girls and is friends with them, although not all the year 10's hangs out with year 12 kids.

I know that Allison's older cousin Lara's coming and she's Marie's best friend and they are the same age and often take Allison and I out, particularly up to The Avenue and the beach if we ask nicely! I like Lara and she was invited by Allison's parents and Marie is glad about that.
I am also looking forward to the party and know that I will have fun, although us lowly grade six kids will not be allowed to hang out with the teenagers if they are outside on the couches or dancing at the reception. The teenagers at those kinds of parties have a lot of fun and enjoy sitting outside on the couches or going outside to talk and hang out away from our parents and do not usually want grade six kids around, but I have an older sister in year 10. Marie and Lara both told Allison and I not to try come hang out with them unless invited. It annoyed me, but I am not surprised.

I am looking forward to the party and Allison and I already talked about tonight's party and said that we will only let kids from our school sit and hang out with us and will not let any scholarship kids join our group tonight. Why they are invited to the party I do not know! Although they are coming to our school next year.

I hope I have fun at the party and my friends and will dance with the boys if they ask, although it is hard with my parents there tonight. All the parents are invited to come tonight, and it is a big family get together to celebrate graduation.

So I headed home to get ready for tonight and relax a bit and said by to my friends for now. I headed home with my parents and Marie.

Chapter 20

Allison

After graduation was over, I headed home with brother Aaron and my parents. We got driven home by our family chauffer and then Aaron and I spent time together for a couple of hours while my parents went out for a coffee before graduation. Our babysitter is looking after us while my parents are out, which is annoying considering. I am 12 years old! So is my brother, but it is only until next year. When we start high school my brother and I will just be on our own after school with the housekeeper.

I know! We are a wealthy family and my parents have always had help around the house as my parents work hard and full-time and mum has worked full time since my brother, and I were 1 years old and that is when she hired our live-in babysitter. We have a separate housekeeper and gardener and a family chauffer.

I had no issues hanging out with my brother Aaron and we get along great and always have. Aaron and I are twins and the same age. We watched a movie and I had changed into tracksuit pants and a t-shirt for now, since it is not comfortable being in a dress at home.

The movie was fun and was a Disney film that we both like. I talked to Aaron and the Housekeeper made us and herself and the live-in babysitter lunch. I will miss my live-in babysitter Tammy next year and I know that Aaron will too. My parents will be dismissing Tammy at the end of the year when we start high school and Tammy is moving to America. My parents think that a housekeeper is enough help in the house for cooking, cleaning, and looking after Aaron and I after school, although when we were little, we needed a live-in babysitter too.

We have a large mansion that is a lot of work for a housekeeper and our housekeeper does all the cooking in the house and helps my parents with catering too, whereas when we were little the live-in babysitter looked after my brother and I and we have always been close to her. My parents said that our housekeeper is enough to help around the house unless they are hosting parties or need catering. They will just hire someone for the night then, a couple of them to help the cook/housekeeper.

I am used to having help around the house! So is my brother. My parents are very wealthy and come from family money and my family is Japanese and overseas our grandparents are wealthy and live oversees and we go to visit every couple of years, and they have been to Australia a few times too.

Oversees my grandparents have a lot of servants in the house and my parents have four people that work for the family. A housekeeper, gardener, live-in babysitter and chauffer. Although next year we will have three. I have not had to clean or pick up my own toys since I was a little and am used to having help around the house and my parents both works hard and own two department stores and several real estate properties and do not just live off family money.

...

Enough on that though! After the movie I went up to my room to get changed for reception dinner that night and knew that I needed to get dressed up. All the families are invited tonight for the graduates. Grade six and year 12 and that is an interesting mix, although Liberty Grammar does this every year.

I got back into my graduation dress. Which was light blue, knee length and very nice! I love my graduation dress. My parents really spoilt me on this one and they got my brother Aaron a suit for graduation, although he's not wearing that tonight. Just black pants and a shirt he said.

I brushed my black hair and just left it out and put some makeup on, since my parents said I can have some light makeup on tonight, but not too much. I just put some lipstick, eyeshadow and foundation on and sprayed some perfume on and got into some low heels. I also added a bracelet and some low heels.

I was ready to go! I went downstairs and my parents and brother were all ready and we got driven to the reception by our family chauffer and we pulled up in front of the reception.

The reception is a wonderful place that is used for a lot of weddings, functions and school or sport events. It is the only function place in our small town, but we are lucky to have this one at least. I have been there quite a bit and know it well.

My parents picked up my cousin Lara on the way and we said hi. Lara wanted to come to the graduation and party and my parents said that that is fine. Lara is my older cousin, and she is 15 years old, and we are close. She looks out for me and my brother at Liberty Grammar and often takes us out. She is close to Leanne's older sister Marie, and they are best friends.

We drove over to the reception and walked in and found our table. We are sitting on the same table as Leanne's parents and sister Marie. It was a table of nine and there was one spare seat, but that was fine, and I am sitting next to Leanne on one side and my brother Aaron on the other and Leanne said hi to me and we talked and ate some bread. I would prefer to be sitting with my friends and not my parents tonight, but we cannot do that at the reception, at least for the grade six kids. The year 12's usually have their own tables separate to their parents.

I was having fun and we ate some bread and had a soft drink and people were still arriving and we could see people coming in and taking their seats.

Marie and Lara had already wandered off and were talking to friends on the other side of the reception before dinner and I know that Lara and Marie are excited to have older kids there and know some year 12 girls anyway, since they are popular in the school. My parents did not have an issue with that and neither did Leanne's. They can see them, and they are just sitting at one of the year 12 tables talking to their friends and will come back for dinner.

I was still on the table with Leanne and Aaron and my parents and Leanne's. I wanted to say hi to friends too but wanted to have something to eat first and was having fun with Leanne anyway and we were talking. Leanne Cummingo is my best friend and we have known each other our whole lives and grew up across the road from each other and have gone to school together too since grade prep.

Leanne is a great friend to me, and I just love her! We are so similar and get along for everything from movies to music, agree on what clothes we like and have all the same friends at school. Leanne's also unofficially second in charge to me in our group at school and is extremely popular at Liberty Grammar. My brother Aaron is talking to Leanne too and gets along great with her. Leanne grew up coming over to my house and often hangs out with my brother and I, although at school Aaron did not play with us girls until this year, but he did not mind at home, likes Leanne, and says that she is great and thinks that she is pretty, which he admitted to me, but Leanne does not know that and at our age I know that nothing would come out of that.

Leanne is pretty though and is the best looking of the girls in our group at school, although I like to think I give her a run for her money and when we get older and start dating boys hopefully, we will both have no trouble getting guys! Although now I am too young for that and my parents would kill me if I said I have a boyfriend at 12 years old, although some of my brothers' friends are cute at school. I particularly like Mitch out of my brother's friends. He is a nice guy, and he is good looking for our age.

Speaking of Mitch! He had found us and had come up to our table to say hi and sat next to Aaron on the other side, since Lara and Marie were sitting with their friends.

Mitch is talking lively to Aaron and said hi to Leanne and me too and we are all hanging out, talking and eating. Mitch is my brother's best friend and lives on the same street as Leanne and I and Mitch is a regular visitor to my house too and I am good friends with Mitch too and so is Leanne.

Other friends had started to wonder over by then and once Ally, Laticia and Monica came over to say hi my parents said it is fine for us to go outside to sit on the couches to talk a bit. They know we will be fine, and it gives the adults a chance to spend some time saying hi to their friends and having a dance before dinner.

I went outside with my friends. There is a front couch area where we like to hang out and so do the older teenagers, away from our parents and I wanted to spend time with my friends and Aaron and Mitch came out to join us girls too with Steve and Michael.

I found a couch to sit on with my friends and was there with my closest friends at school. Leanne, Ally, Laticia and Monica and the boys Aaron, Mitch, Steven, Aaden, and Michael were on the other couch.

I was having fun with my friends, and we took advantage of there being no teenagers outside now. They usually like to sit on the couches but are currently inside.

We do not usually dance or if we do it is when we like the song or if our parents force us. I was talking to Leanne and Ally on either side of me. I love Leanne. We are close, and

Ally is also one of my closest friends. We all grew up together. The boys were sitting across from us and look like they are having fun too. Making a loud group. I do not mind having the boys outside and neither do my friends. A couple of them are cute actually! Out of the boys group.

I am starting to notice boys and so are my friends. I am at the end of primary school and nearly a teenager at 12 years old. Although until last year there was a clear boy's group and girls' group at school in the popular crowd. I like my male friends this year and so do the rest of the girls, but no-one has been asked out yet and we are a bit young for that anyway. My parents would kill me! If I had a boyfriend this young. They can be strict.

...

I was still sitting on the couch with Leanne, Ally, Laticia, and Monica when who should walk out but Anni, Sierra, Alexa and Melanie from Jefferson primary school and Shane, who is like of the girls from what we hear and got the dance scholarship.
Here we go. Seriously! They are brave to come out here and should know better when the popular Liberty Grammar kids are out on the couches, although coming from another school they would not know that.

I particularly know who Sierra is and Melanie and Alexa and so does Leanne. Since they used to be part of Sabrina Brewers group at school until they got kicked out for taking the Liberty Grammar scholarships.

I know all this and so does Leanne and my other friends. Sabrina told me. Although I would not want that to get out to too many people.

It is not that Sabrina, and I are friends or anything. Far from it. We hate each other! It started when we met at The Avenue and got into an argument. I have become increasingly aware of Sabrina Brewer and her friends and know how popular Sabrina is at her school and that she is the ringleader of the group and Sabrina in turn knows about our group.

I do not know! It is getting to point now where I am starting to think about doing something about Sabrina Brewer and her idiot friends and talk to Leanne and my other friends about it all the time. Leanne agrees with me to a point, but also agrees that nothing official will be done until we start high school. My friends and I want to make a splash in high school, and I think that Sabrina does too, from what we hear.

I looked at my friends and then at Anni, Sierra, Alexa, Melanie, and Shane. I am annoyed with all those Jefferson primary school kids, just like Sabrina Brewer is. I do not think that the Jefferson primary school kids look happy to see us and did not realise we would be out here. The whole popular group is out in the lobby right now and everyone knows that I am not to be messed with at my school and Jefferson primary school too.

I was not going to be hitting anyone tonight and neither are my friends, although I would hit someone that messes with me and so would Leanne. We have that reputation! At my school and Jefferson primary school, after my Leanne's with Stacey Green. That fight really was a surprise to Leanne and Stacey and they went for it from what I here!

It was my first cat fight with anyone, and Leanne cannot stand that stupid bimbo Stacey Green as much as I cannot stand Sabrina Brewer.

It is just these Jefferson primary school kids! Seriously. I cannot believe that before this year we have had no trouble with that school and now this year, wow! It has gone time between our two schools and what is going to happen next year? Who knows, but Leanne and I both agree it might be bad and we need to do something about it.
Anyway. So Anni, Sierra, Alexa, Melanie, and Shane had come out and knew it was too late to go back in, we had spotted them, and I got up off the couch anyway and so Allison, Ally, Laticia, and Monica. No-one is happy with this lot now! They are unpopular at our school and at their old school.

To my surprise Sierra did not back down and just walk into the lobby, followed by her friends and I reacted quickly too that and spoke.

"Would you lot go back inside! This is for popular kids only out here in the lobby."

Sierra did not back down to that and spoke.

"What do you mean unpopular? We have not even started at this school yet."
I chipped in after that one and spoke.
"Scholarship kids are always unpopular at our school. Should have stayed at Jefferson primary guys."

"Scholarship kids are always unpopular at our school. Should have stayed at Jefferson primary guys."

Of course, there was an argument after that! The Jefferson primary school kids were feisty, I will give them that and I was joining the arguing with my friends, and we needed to let these idiots know what is going on and who is in charge. Leanne, Ally, Laticia, and Monica were all arguing too.

Our argument was cut short though, by my cousin Lara and Leanne's sister Marie coming out to again find Leanne and I in a shouting match with the Jefferson primary kids, like at The Avenue.

Marie and Lara were not happy with Leanne and I and or friends. They came out and it was not just them. Marie and Lara had been hanging out with some year 12 girls and boys too and look like they have been having fun. Marie and Lara are extremely popular at school and have friends in year 12 which is a huge statement with year 10 kids. Year 12's only talk to the extremely popular kids from younger grades.

Marie and Lara walked into the lobby with their friends and found Leanne and I in another argument with Jefferson Secondary College kids. They were not happy about it at all.

Marie came up and broke up the argument and so did Lara and I know that I was embarrassing my cousin and Marie and so was Leanne in front of their year 12 friends, and they were not happy, although they looked annoyed at the Jefferson primary school kids too.

I did stop arguing and so did Leanne and my other friends. Marie and Lara told us to go back inside, my parents want me back and so does Leanne's parents and the boys came back with us and our other friends.

...

Once inside the reception the night was a lot more fun, and we were no longer able to go out to the lobby. The teenagers had taken over that and I had not seen Lara or Marie all night since they broke up the argument. They are having fun with their friends, and I know that I will hear all about it tomorrow.

Leanne and I stuck away from the Jefferson Primary school kids and stuck with our own friends and are having a lot of fun. We even got up to dance and danced with the boys for fun, although it did not mean anything serious at our age and my parents did not mind. They can see us, and it is all very innocent. Just dancing.

I danced with Mitch and Aaron danced with Leanne, which is fine. Ally, Laticia, and Monica got asked by Steve, Aaden, and Michael. This was my first dance with a boy and my friends too and it was awkward at first, but I put my arms around his neck and his on my waist.

Our parents were embarrassing my friends and I though and got excited to see the boys and girls dancing together and said that we are cute. My parents took a photo of Mitch and I dancing together, and we grinned at each other. It was funny. They took one of Aaron and Leanne too. I was having fun with Mitch and had no issues with dancing with him. I knew that my brother did not mind either as he is dancing with Leanne. I know that Aaron has a bit of a crush on Leanne and is glad that she agreed to dance with him. I do not know if Aaron will ask Leanne out as we grow up, but now they are just friends. Mitch and I are also just friends, although he is cute.

We danced to a couple of songs with the boys and then they played some retro tracks and we all got into it and Marie and Lara, and the rest of the teenagers came back out and we all danced and had some fun. Marie and Lara were dancing with year 12 boys and that is why they were out in the lobby all night, to hang out with the cute guys. It was a fun night for everyone, and graduation is officially over!

Part 4-School code in the works

The idea

Chapter 21

Stacey

I cannot believe that primary school is officially over and neither can my friends. We are in high school next year! I can't believe it.

I did pretty well with my grades and sport and my parents are proud of the awards that I won at graduation, but said that they want me to concentrate on my study next year too, although they know how much I love sport.

My friends and I are all doing well and are looking forward to summer holidays. We have six weeks off until we start year 7 next year and I am happy to be starting high school with my closest friends Robert, Shannon and David and joining us next year is Anna! I cannot believe it and am excited about it and so are my friends. Anna went to Rydal primary school last year, but we have been playing basketball together for years and are good friends and Anna is planning to come to Jefferson Secondary for high school and wants too. She asked her parents to let her, and it is not hard to transfer schools. Anna lives in the town over, but there is a direct bus for school students.

…

On Saturday afternoon I went over to Robert's house and so did Shannon and David. We are planning to hang out and go to The Avenue, then the beach and come back to Robert's place to have a movie night and I cleared all this with my parents, and they are fine with it, and I am just not allowed to stay at Robert's house too late and his parents and little brother Sal will be there anyway.

I usually hang out with my friends on the weekends and rarely spend time on my own. Robert, Shannon and I have been inseparable since we were babies and I have grown up going to their houses and them to mine. David is the same. He spends most of his weekends with Robert, Shannon and I and our whole group is super close and we live near each other. Anna can't come this week, but I would have invited her too. She's out with her parents.

I got up around 10:00am and had breakfast with my parents. I am on holidays now! So, no basketball, swimming or any homework on the weekends and I like to sleep in and my parents let me. Mum and I had breakfast together, since dad is at work. He sometimes works weekends and is a lawyer, so he works some crazy hours, but he likes what he does.

Mum is working today too and is glad that I am off with my friends today and will drive me over to the beach.

Mum is a wedding photographer and does all sorts of other photography too, for people in our small town. Mum is doing a wedding today, with the help of an assistant.

So, I had some cereal and juice and was still in my pyjama's, but I had a shower straight after breakfast and got into some beach clothes. I brushed out my blond hair and I have very blond hair! Trust me and it is all natural. I take after my mum and my dad and my mum was as blond as me as kid and her teenage years and still has blond hair, although now it is darker than mine and mixed with greys.
I have blond hair, blue eyes, and very fair skin, although when I am out in the Queensland sun, I get a bit tan, but I usually must be very sun conscious because it is easy for my skin to burn. My mum is Irish and so are my grandparents. That is where the blond hair comes from! My dad is French and has blue eyes and light brown hair.

I like my blond hair and hope that I keep it and it does not get darker, although I have been told by older friends that blond hair gets darker when I go through puberty and so forth.

I am also very tall for my age and at 12 years old tower over most of the girls in my class and the boys too, although that will change in high school, I think. Girls get their growth spurts first then boys, my mum said.

I am already 5"6 tall and believe that I am still growing and so do my parents. I have grown three inches this year alone. I am very tall for a girl and take after my parents. Mum is very tall at 5"11 and dad is 6"4, so I had no chance! Trust me and mum thinks that I might grow to her height or taller the next couple of years. I hope not! I do not want to be too tall, although judging from my parents I will be.

I do not know! I certainly tower over Shannon. That is for sure. She is tiny at 5"0 tall and I do not think that Shannon will get much taller than that, but we will see. Robert and I are the same height, which I think might embarrass him and David is taller than me and is the tallest guy in our class and David is still growing and is the tallest guy in grade six and Sabrina Brewer and I are the tallest girls in grade six. Robert, I think will get taller in high school. He is only 12 years old! Robert's grown a lot the last couple of years and used to be shorter than me, but he is grown a lot the last couple of years and seems to have shot up overnight and so has David.

Enough on that though. I dried my hair and put it back in a ponytail and then got changed into a red one-piece bathing suit, some shorts, a t-shirt, thongs and had sunglasses perched on top of my hair. I also brought a change of clothes in a beach bag, since we are going to Robert's house later and I can have a shower at the beach change rooms.

Mum drove me over to the beach and I found Robert and Shannon there with their mums and David, but my mum just said hi and then left me with them and rushed off to work and Robert and Shannon's mum are going to lunch and leaving us at the beach for a while on our own. They are starting to trust us a bit more now, but our mum's can see us from the beach café they will be at anyway if they want to.

I headed down to the beach with my friends and love the beach, I always have. We come to the beach all the time. I got out my towel, took my shorts and t-shirt off and had my bathers on and Shannon had a similar one-piece bathing suit. Neither of us like wearing bikinis.

I had fun at the beach with my friends and we went swimming and ate some lunch our mum's packed, sun-baked a bit and talked too. We stayed at the beach for ages, 3 hours and went swimming and watched the surfers too and they look so cool! I would love to learn how to surf and so do my friends, but my parents said next year, since I am already swimming and playing basketball. I am very sporty! Definitely.

After we finished at the beach, I headed up to the changerooms. Shannon and Robert's mums are waiting for us and it is easier to get changed at the beach. I had a shower and got changed into some jeans and a t-shirt and pulled my hair back in a ponytail. I talked to Shannon and came out and we were both ready and so were the boys.

We met the mums at the café after that and we ordered some takeaway ice cream and they paid for the meal. We took the ice cream back to Robert's house and Shannon's mum said bye to us and she headed home as we are going to Robert's house tonight and his parents are looking after us. Shannon's mum just came for lunch to keep Robert's mum company today. She is picking Shannon up later from Robert's house. We are staying for dinner too and Robert's parents are hosting tonight, and I do not mind. I love Robert's parents and little brother Sal and always have fun at his house and so do my friends.

…

Once I got to Robert's house and so did my friends, Robert's little brother Sal came running up and gave me a hug and Shannon too and David ruffled his hair and then Robert said hello to his little brother, and we all went into the living room.

I adore Sal! So do my friends. He is so adorable, and Robert is the only one of my friends that has a younger sibling, although David has an older brother Shane, who we all like. He is in high school.

Sal just turned 4 years old and is a lot younger than Robert, by eight years. He is a mini-Robert and looks like him, which is cute, and Sal has dark curly hair, brown eyes and olive skin and is a ridiculously cute little boy and everyone adores him in my group of friends and my parents love Sal too and spoil him rotten if Robert brings him over or we go to visit.

I am an only child and would have loved a little brother or sister growing up, but my parents cannot have more kids and looks like I will be the only daughter! As a result, I am spoilt by my parents. They always say that I was their miracle baby and my parents hoped for another baby, but it did not happen for them. Shannon is an only child too.

...

Enough on that though! I was having fun with my friends and Robert's parents ordered dinner and got some movies for us. I like a movie night. It is fun and I often do that with my friends. We put on a comedy that we all enjoy, and Robert's parent's and Sal watched it with us. We were having fun and laughed at the antics of the lead, who we all like.

After the movie I just spent time together with my friends. We had a fun night playing some games and got on the video games, which we all like doing. I had a good night and headed home after my dad picked me up.

Chapter 22

Sabrina

School holidays are here! I am looking forward to a break from school and hanging out with my friends at the beach. The group has gotten smaller since school finished and several of my friends are going to a different school next year. My main friends leaving are Grace and Sophie and I am really going to miss them when they go to Rydal Secondary College next year. We are close friends. Elise also goes to the same school, and we are also good friends.

Grace and Sophie are also moving to the other town, as their parents are opening a shop in that town and want to be close to their work and enroll the girls in school there to be closer to their work and home. Elise is still living in a farmhouse between the two towns and has decided to go to Rydal Secondary College when her parents asked her what school she wants to go to for high school. For all the sports they have to offer.

I will miss my friends, but the group going to Jefferson Secondary College is one I am happy with, and we are all close. All of us girls and the boys too. Emma, Vicky, and Charlotte are coming to school with me and so are Matt, Peter, Sam and Alan from the group and I know that

Stacey Green and her friends Robert, Shannon and David are all coming to school with us too.

I am happy with my group, but I will miss Grace, Sophie and Elise and so will my friends. Our group has been joined at the hip right through primary school. It will be different without them next year.

High school is a whole new ballgame to primary school, and I know that and have even talked to my sisters about it. Monica promised to look out for me next year and show me the ropes of Jefferson Secondary College. Monica will be in year 11 next year and I will be a lowly year 7 next year and so will my friends. Not like in primary school, where we were the big kids.

Having a sister in year 11 will help me out and my friends and I know that. My oldest sister Sandra will not be at school with me next year. Sandra graduated from high school this year and is starting a teaching degree in a couple of months and says that she cannot wait to be out of high school, as year 12 was tough. Sandra did well at school last year though and got great grades and graduated with high enough grades to go to university to study teaching. Sandra loves kids and is looking forward to university next year. My parents are proud of Sandra and happy that she got into university. They also like that Sandra does not give them too much trouble during her high school years.

They worry a lot more about Monica. Monica is not as serious about school and does not have great grades. They keep reminding her to study and keep her grades up, as she is in year 11 this year, but Monica hates school and prefers to hang out with her friends. Monica wanted to drop out of high school last year and find a job. She can do that from year 10, but my parents were furious about it and said that they want her to at least finish year 11 and 12 and then she can find work or continue to study. Monica is still at school now, but she is planning to get a casual job this year to earn her own money. Sandra has also had a part-time job in a retail shop since she was 15 years old.

Sandra is still dating her boyfriend Michael and Michael also graduated this year and is going to university next year to do engineering and he is very smart. Sandra and Michael got into the same university and are happy about it and are serious about each other, although they are young at 18 years old.

Sandra is still going to live at home with my parents and sisters and I next year and cannot afford to move out just yet as she is going to university next year and my parents do not want Sandra moving in with Michael so young and are old fashioned that way. Sandra does not mind that and neither do my parents. Sandra helps my parents a lot and they appreciate everything she does to help. She especially helps with babysitting at the house, particularly looking after my little sister Alana. Sandra babysits me too and oversees the home during the week until my parents get home from work. Sandra does not babysit every day but. That is not fair to her. Since Sandra works, has a boyfriend and a part-time job in a store. If Sandra cannot babysit then Monica's in charge and expected to babysit, although Monica hates being asked to do that on Friday and Saturday nights, but she must if Sandra cannot babysit.

Sandra has not paid rent yet, as she will be at university next year and my parents will not expect her to until she works full-time. They say that to all of us and I know that in high school I will be expected to look after Alana when my sisters are not available too.

My sister Monica is quite different to Sandra and Monica and Sandra do not always get along very well, although as sisters they do respect each other to a point, but you should see the arguments they get into at home! When Sandra wants to go out with her boyfriend Michael and cannot babysit and Monica then must babysit or if Sandra tells Monica off when she is caught drinking or smoking before or if something happens at school that affects Sandra.

Sandra's the older sister! In that regard and is more responsible than Monica and my parents trust her more. I love my big sister Sandra and look up to her. She is a neat big sister to have and really looks after me and we talk a lot and I also like Sandra's boyfriend Michael too. He is great and is like one of the family and Sandra's introduced Michael to my parents and they adore him, and so do Alana and I. and Monica like Michael too and gets along with him well. Sandra and Michael are serious about each other and have been going out for ages, although they are still young and not looking to go too far with their relationship. Moving in together comes later.

Monica is 16 years old, and we will be only 3 years apart when I turn 13 years old next month. I am going to be a teenager soon like my sisters and am looking forward to it. Monica and I get along great and are friends as well as sisters and Monica looks out for me a lot and we talk a lot and I know more about what Monica does than my parents or Sandra do and would never say anything to them. Monica's the cheekier one out of my older sisters and she drinks at parties and sometimes vapes too and if my parents knew that they would kill her! Monica also has a guy she likes. Whose name is Dan, and they are still "seeing each other." Dan has not asked Monica out or met my parents yet, although I have met him, and Sandra and Michael know Dan from seeing him with Monica at The Avenue.

Monica can be a troublemaker at school and causes a lot of strife for my parents and does not do much homework, is always getting into arguments and sometimes even skips classes with her friends and got suspended last year for two days for getting into a fist fight on school grounds.

I do not know! My parents say that they are at their wits end with Monica and are sick of the trouble at school and went nuts over the fight and getting suspended last year.

In Monica's defense though that fight was not really her fault and was started by Marie from Liberty Grammar and Lara and they got into it after an argument went too far. Monica does not regret the fight, although my parents were super angry over it and Monica has not gotten into another punch on with Marie, although she said that if she starts her again, she might and warned me many times over the Liberty Grammar girls. So has Sandra, although Sandra just sticks away from them and does not cause trouble. Sandra's not a troublemaker, but does not like Liberty Grammar kids either, no-one in my neighborhood does. Who could stand those snobs!

The Liberty grammar kids are idiots. Allison Ritz and Leanne Cummingo are not any better than Lara or Monica. They are both my age and Leanne is Marie's younger sister and Allison is Lara's younger cousin.

I can tell that Monica is worried about my friends and I and so are her friends and Monica has warned me many times to stay away from Liberty Grammar and particularly away from Allison and Leanne. Monica calls those two mini versions of Lara and Marie and says that they are not any better than them and I agree with her. I cannot stand those two idiots! Neither can any of my friends.

Marie and Lara leave me alone and Marie and Lara leave Allison and Leanne alone. Monica said that she would never go around picking on kids 3 years younger than her and Marie and Lara repeated the same things about my friends and I. Although Marie has been getting into a lot more arguments with Marie since that incident at The Avenue and keeps warning me to stay away from Allison and Leanne.

I do not know! My friends and I have started to get worried about what is going to happen next year between the schools and agree that something needs to be done, but I am not sure what. The idea of having to talk to that witch Allison Ritz or her crony Leanne Cummingo pisses me off already and I think that Allison and I would be in an argument in five minutes and if she ever hit me I would not back away either, although that thankfully has not happened. We will see what happens! Something should be done though.

Chapter 23

Allison

On Monday afternoon I was spending time together with my best friend Leanne at home and my mum had gone out and dad were at work, so we were being looked after by my live-in babysitter and housekeeper.

My live-in babysitter Tammy will not be with us for long now and is leaving to go to America in two weeks. Tammy is heading out overseas for work and study and said that she will be working as a live-in-babysitter overseas for a family with kids that are still all under 5 years old. One is a baby at 1 year old and the other kid is 3 years old. Tammy is going to America to study while she works and is looking forward to her adventure.

I will miss Tammy and so will my brother Aaron. Tammy is the youngest of our help in the house and has looked after my brother and I since she was 18 years old, and we were babies at 1 year old. Tammy is still young at 30 years old now, but my brother and I do not need a live-in babysitter or a housekeeper anymore. At least my parents do not think that we do. My parents love Tammy though and wish her well. They are sending her off with references, a big pay cheque and telling her to stay in touch with us and I know our housekeeper will miss her too as they are close friends and Tammy is a big help for our housekeeper too.

I am on school holidays now and am looking forward to two months of no school and hanging out with my friends and brother and cousin Lara, but I am going away with my parents and Aaron in two weeks to Sydney. We are going to Sydney for Christmas and new year, and we have family in Sydney. Both my dad's sisters live there with their families. Lara's family is in Queensland with us, and we have family in Japan and America too.

It is always fun to go to Sydney for the holidays or overseas. I have family in Sydney, cousins, aunts, and uncles, although my grandparents live overseas and my second cousins. My grandparents are coming to Sydney too to visit all the way to Australia, and they are travelling with my aunt and uncle. It will be a big family Christmas and I am looking forward to it and know that it will be fun, and I am looking forward to seeing my Japanese grandparents. They are still young enough to travel and enjoy visiting Australia and the family and we visit Japan once every two years to visit them too. I know that I will have fun with my cousins and am looking forward to catching up with the family.

It is always fun going down to Sydney to visit my cousins, grandparents and aunts and uncles and my brother and I are always spoilt by everyone because we are youngest in the family and the only kids in primary school still and we get presents from everyone in the family, although that stops when we start high school next year and then my parents said that we will just have a big kk with the family to make sure that everyone gets a present.

Anyway, so other than the Sydney trip I will spend most of the holiday hanging out with my friends and we enjoy going to the beach and the movies and going out to the shops on The Avenue. Every year mine or my friends' parents always try to take a few of mine and my brother's friends down to the Gold Coast to one of the theme parks.

The Gold coast is not exactly close to my town, it is about a two-hour drive, although it is easy to get to and my parents take me out to the Gold Coast often for dinner and nights out and we try to go to the theme parks often too.

It is nice of the parents to take us down there and they do a group trip like this every year. Every year two sets of parents take us, and we are going this year with my parents and Leanne's and my whole group is going from school. Ally, Laticia and Monica and my brothers/my friends Aaron, Mitch, three of the other friends.

We always have a lot of fun, and I am looking forward to when I will be allowed to go down to the Gold Coast without my parents, but it will not be for a while, not until I am well into my teens. As it takes 2 hours by train to get there, and we are too young to go on our own.

...

So that is my plan for fun this summer! I am looking forward to my trips and so are my family and friends, but I know, and my friends know that there is the potential to have trouble this summer too and going into year 7 and high school next year and I have already talked at length about it with Leanne and Laticia, Ally, and Monica.

Trouble comes in the form of a certain blond named Sabrina Brewer and I know it and so do my friends and not just Sabrina, but her friends too and I am particularly worried about Sabrina's friends that are going to Jefferson Secondary College with her, as we'll rarely see Elise or Grace and Sophie once they go to school at Rydal Secondary College in the other town, as we have a lot more contact and trouble with Jefferson Secondary College at my school and I know it and my cousin Lara has warned me already to keep away from the kids from Jefferson Secondary College and Leanne's sister Marie said exactly the same thing too.

I know Sabrina Brewer is trouble and so do my friends. Sabrina is the ringleader of the group and the loudest and most obnoxious and she enjoys getting into arguments, or it seems like it because we have had a couple of screaming matches and Sabrina is as bad as me in an argument.

I get on Sabrina's nerves, and she gets on mine, and we have quickly hated each other this year.
Anyway, I was talking to Leanne and hanging out, when I decided to bring something up with her that I had been thinking about and planning, without talking to my friends yet.

I have been thinking of starting an elite group next year when we start high school next year. All the girls need to be the most popular girls from primary school and wealthy, popular and friends with Leanne and me. I have been thinking about this for a couple of months now, since I met Sabrina, that we need to have some sort of protection in high school from public school kids like Sabrina and her friends.

I am not sure what Leanne will think of my idea, I am hoping she will help me set up my new group and be my second in charge, since we are best friends already and Leanne is a leader in the group too and extremely popular at my school and cannot stand public school kids.

I mentioned my idea to Leanne, and she was interested straight away and asked me a dozen questions. First one being who should we have in the group. We both agreed that Ally, Laticia, and Monica are the obvious choices if they agree and want to do it and that we do not want boys. We want to keep the main group small, but might think about adding other kids to it, particularly if we want us to be established as leaders in year 7.

I have even thought of a name, although Leanne needs to agree and so do my other friends. The stars sound good and maybe the other group not made up of Ally, Laticia and Monica could be stars, if we can get any to agree.

I do not know! Leanne and I talked all afternoon and started planning but had no idea how our idea was about to take off in year 7!

Chapter 24

Sabrina

On Saturday afternoon I was spending time together with my friends Emma, Vicky, Amy, and Charlotte at the park, since it is summer, and we are off school and dancing too. I am looking forward to the summer holidays and hanging out with my friends and my friends and I have the summer booked.

I am going away with my parents for a week and Alana to the Gold Coast in a couple of weeks. My older sisters are not coming. Sandra said that she wants to stay in our hometown and spend time with Michael and her friends and my parents are fine with that, and that Sandra is old enough and responsible enough to look after our house and herself for a couple of weeks. Sandra's been talking about what she is going to do while we are away and is looking forward to it.

Monica's staying home with Sandra too and not coming to the Gold Coast. Monica's sixteen years old now and wants to hang out with her friends and Dan and like she said we have the beach in our hometown anyway. My parents only agreed to let Monica stay home as they know that Sandra and Michael will keep an eye on her. Monica has promised my parents that she will behave.

I am going to the Gold Coast with my parents and Alana and am not allowed to stay home with my older sisters. My parents said that I am too young, and I do not mind going on holiday for a week. The Gold Coast is not far from my hometown. Only 2 hours by car and my parents book a beach apartment and plan to take my little sister and I sightseeing, the theme parks and beach.

It is only for a week, and I am looking forward to coming back to my hometown after that and spending time with my friends and then starting high school next year.

...

My friends and I were spending time together on the playground. Just Emma, Vicky, Charlotte, Amy, and me.

Our group seems to have shrunk since primary school finished and these are my closest friends that are coming to Jefferson Secondary College with me next year. Grace and Sophie have already moved to the other town and Elise too is moving to Rydall Secondary College with Grace and Sophie.

Emma, Vicky, Charlotte, Amy, and I are already a close-knit group and I love all my friends, although I am the unannounced leader of my group and I expect my friends to listen to me and to make sure that they do not go against the group decisions.
I was still spending time together with my friends when I realized that Allison Ritz had just got out of her family limousine and Leanne Cummingo was with her. Along with their friends Ally, Laticia, and Monica.

I nearly groaned aloud, and my friends were annoyed too. Can't those idiots leave us alone? Honestly. Allison Ritz is the last person I want to see. At least I had my friends with me though.

I waited for Allison. She is clearly heading right for my friends and I and so is Leanne and their friends. I am not scared of Allison, I waited for her, and wondered what she wanted. Allison did not try to start an argument with me for once and walked right up to my group like she is a friend of ours and said hi to me!
I was completely shocked and so were my friends. Is Allison Ritz trying to be friendly with me? Seriously after the two arguments we had. That would be a first. I was not going to start an argument with Allison though right then

if she is trying to be friendly, although I do not like her or her friends.

I said hi back to Allison, feeling very awkward, wondering what she wants and curious. So were my friends. Allison said that she wants to talk to me about an idea she had.

An idea? What idea? Why would I want to be involved in anything that Allison has thought up or her friends? Allison introduced her friends as stars for the first time and said that she is planning to run the group in high school with Leanne's help and that her other friends are keen to be involved with the stars too.

What are stars? I was amused. It was the stupidest idea I have heard so far, and I had no idea why Allison came up to my friends and I and introduced her friends as stars. It is obviously a clique of some kind for high school. Involving Liberty Grammar girls.
I was amused and so were my friends and I had no idea what stars were, but Allison was quick to explain that the stars she hoped were going to be the most popular group at school next year and that her and Leanne want to make a big splash in high school and impress the older kids and want to make their group the most popular kids in school and were not going to let any scholarship kids into the group.

Why is Allison talking to me about this? The stars are obviously aimed at Liberty Grammar kids or year 7 girls, Allison said that boys were not going to be involved. I just nodded at Allison and wondered when she was going to leave me alone. Why would I care about some stupid clique she is trying to start at Liberty Grammar in year 7?

I listened to Allison explain about her idea quite patiently considering that I hate her and Leanne Cummingo and finally had enough. I boldly asked why she is talking to my friends and I about this idea. Is she under the impression that my friends and I want to join her stupid clique? Allison mentioned that any girls not actually stars will be called starlets and are considered followers to the stars.

Emma, Vicky, Charlotte, and Amy laughed at my comment and Allison looked annoyed, but also knew she had to get to the point quickly or there would be trouble, as both groups were there.

Allison was quick to say that no way are my friends and I going to be involved in the stars or starlets. Those groups are private school girls only and not scholarship kids. Of course! I was not surprised at all and really annoyed about this. Typical Allison and Leanne and their friends only letting rich kids into the popular group. I would not expect anything less. Not that I would want to join their stupid group.

Allison saw that I got annoyed at that comment about rich kids only being let into the stars and finally got to the point of why she wants to talk to me.

Allison asked me if I would be interested in joining the school code as they are going to call the whole thing, but not as a star or starlet, but to head a rival public school group to the stars.

Oh my God! Why didn't I think of it? What a great idea. It is perfect and what I have been looking to do anyway. I am just as keen as Allison Ritz to make a big splash in high school and be popular and I hate private school kids. Allison flattered me a bit to a point to say that her and Leanne thought of me straight away to be a leader in the school code and could tell that I am a leader among the public-school kids.

I was flattered and excited by the idea and so were my friends. Emma, Vicky, Charlotte, and Amy were listening to them and seemed keen. Well, if I do decide to start a group like that in high school, I need my friends to be involved too. Especially as Allison and Leanne already have stars. Ally, Laticia, and Monica by the looks of it. The groups matched exactly.

I asked Allison about her idea, a dozen questions. It is her idea, but if she wants me to be involved and be a leader in the school code then we need to work together to a point to start the whole thing and start recruiting other girls to get involved. Allison made it clear to me though that she has no interest in being friends with me and neither does Leanne or her other friends. In fact, Allison said that she cannot stand my friends and I and is sick of all the arguments and trouble this year and thinks that if we are going to hate each other why not make it official and start rival groups in high school. Allison said that she could have just started stars but thinks that it would be more fun to have a rival group to be competition for the stars.

I feel exactly the same way as Allison and told her that I hate her too and can't wait to be competition for her in high school and I am going to make my own group with only public school girls to be a rival group to the stars and

Emma, Vicky, Charlotte and Amy were very quick to say that they want to be involved. So that was easy! At least finding friends to join my group, but what group? I didn't even know what I was going to call my clique in year 7 and Allison asked me if I have any ideas of what I want to call the group. It has to be completely different to the stars. I talked to my friends and said that I'd be back forming a huddle with Vicky, Charlotte, Emma and Amy. We had a name after talking about it and before going back to Allison and Leanne and their friends. We did a group shout.

"Unicorns rock!"

I loved the name and the sound of it and my friends and I all loved it and were starting to feel like a group already. We were anyway and in high school this would be my new group. Unicorn followers would be called larks.

I feel exactly the same way as Allison and told her that I hate her too and can't wait to be competition for her in high school and I am going to make my own group with only public-school girls to be a rival group to the stars and Emma, Vicky, Charlotte and Amy were very quick to say that they want to be involved. So that was easy! At least finding friends to join my group, but what group? I did not even know what I was going to call my clique in year 7 and Allison asked me if I had any ideas of what I wanted to call the group. It must be completely different to the stars. I talked to my friends and said that I would be back forming a huddle with Vicky, Charlotte, Emma, and Amy. We had a name after talking about it and before going back to Allison and Leanne and their friends. We did a group shout.

"Unicorns rock!"

I loved the name and the sound of it and my friends, and I all loved it and were starting to feel like a group already. We were anyway and in high school this would be my new group. Unicorn followers would be called larks.
I went back to Allison and Allison knew the name of the group anyway from all the shouting going on and looked amused and told me that it was the stupidest name for a group she'd ever heard, but she has no say in my groups name or anything else to do with the unicorns and we've already agreed to that.
So, Allison and I had our groups, group names and friends that have agreed to join the stars and the unicorns, now the real work was about to begin in year 7. School code here we come!

 The End

Stay tuned for the exiting sequel.
School code kids' year 7-Start of the school code